SCHOOLS
AND PARENTS

John Partington

and Ted Wragg

Cassell

CASSELL

Cassell Educational Limited
Artillery House
Artillery Row
London SW1 1RT

Copyright © Cassell Educational Limited 1989

First published 1989

ISBN 0-304-31714-4 (hardback)
0-304-31712-8 (paperback)

British Library Cataloguing in Publication Data
Partington, J.A. (John A.)
    Schools and parents. – (Education matters)
    1. Great Britain. Schools – For children
    I. Title II. Wragg, Ted III. Series
    371′.00941

Typeset by Input Typesetting Ltd, London

Printed and bound in Great Britain by
Biddles Ltd., Guildford and King's Lynn.

CONTENTS

FOREWORD

Professor E. C. Wragg, Exeter University

During the 1980s a succession of Education Acts changed considerably the nature of schools and their relationships with the outside world. Parents in particular were given more rights and responsibilities, including the opportunity to serve on the governing body of their child's school. The 1988 Education Reform Act in particular, by introducing for the first time a National Curriculum, the testing of children at the ages of 7, 11, 14 and 16, local management, including financial responsibility and the creation of new types of school, was a radical break with the past.

In the wake of such rapid and substantial changes it was not just parents and lay people, but also teachers and other professionals working in education, who found themselves struggling to keep up with what these many changes meant and how to get the best out of them. The *Education Matters* series addresses directly the major topics of reform, such as the new curriculum, testing and assessment, the role of parents and the handling of school finances, considering their effects on both primary and secondary education.

The aim of the series is to present information about the challenges facing education in the remainder of the twentieth century in an authoritative but readable form. The books in the series, therefore, are of particular interest to parents, governors and all those interested in education, but are written in such a way as to give an overview to student and experienced teachers or other professionals in the field.

Each book gives an account of the relevant legislation and background, but, more importantly, stresses the practical implications of change with specific examples of what is being or can be done to make reforms work effectively. The authors of each book are not only authorities in their field, but also have direct experience of the matters they write about, and that is why the *Education Matters* series makes an important contribution to both debate and practice.

INTRODUCTION

Twenty-odd years ago there was an important turning-point in education. The 1967 Plowden Report, a government inquiry into primary schools, actually devoted a whole chapter to the importance of parents. The research it had undertaken showed that parents' attitudes strongly influenced their children's progress in school.

Before that time, parents were not always welcome, and some schools were notorious for having a white line painted in the playground with a sign saying that parents should not proceed beyond it. One head even wrote to them saying that their sole duty was to bring their children to school clean and ready for work. Under no circumstances should they ever enter the school yard. At its worst it was almost as if being a parent were something to be ashamed of, certainly not the sort of thing you admitted to your friends.

During the 1970s many schools became much more welcoming. Some set up Parent–Teacher Associations (PTAs), most held open days or parents' evenings. It became more common, especially in primary schools, to see parents helping in classrooms or on school trips. At a primary school in Cornwall, the head caused quite a stir by actually writing to parents asking if they had any expertise in needlework, cookery, country dancing or anything that would be of interest to the school. His biggest coup was persuading a retired bank manager to collect the dinner money.

One of the greatest problems which parents report is sheer ignorance of what goes on in school. They find out little from their own children, who are often reluctant to discuss their day once it is over. In reality, the head may have shot himself, the senior mistress run off with the caretaker, and the school burned down, but ask the average 12-year-old what had happened at school that day and most would say cheerily, 'Nothing much, same as usual', before trotting off to play with their friends, do their homework or watch television.

1

Despite the increased rights parents have acquired from the 1980, 1981, 1986 and 1988 Education Acts, many individual parents still feel impotent. Several of the extra rights and powers, such as participating in the selection of staff, taking responsibility for budgets, overseeing the conduct and curriculum of the school, only apply to parents who are governors. Most parents do not seek to play a dominant role in the running of their child's school and some are extremely reluctant to volunteer to be a parent-governor.

It is easy to assume that, because the powers of school governors have increased, individual parents are now well catered for and have no further needs. Yet their position is still weaker than that of parents in some other places, such as Scandinavia, where there is more of an obligation on schools to make parents part of a three-way contract with teachers and children themselves when, for example, an important decision about a pupil's future has to be made.

One of us remembers vividly our own first-ever parents' evening when we all waited in line eager to find out why we had sent so many Vim containers to school, only for them to be brought home painted purple with rice crispies stuck on and labelled 'Star Ship Enterprise' or 'Kevin Keegan'. When the teacher told the first mother in the queue that her daugher was 'very slow' we all suddenly developed a great interest in the ceiling and our shoe-laces, fearful of what was in store for us.

We have written this book, therefore, for parents and those who work with them or want to know more about the sort of role that parents can play in schools following the various Education Acts of the 1980s. In Chapters 1 and 2 we describe the rights and powers that parents and children have acquired. In Chapter 3, conscious that schools for many parents are places of deep mystery, we explain how they work. In Chapter 4 we show how parents can get involved in their children's education without being excessively pushy or trying to take over the school. Finally, we deal in Chapter 5 with the sort of questions that parents have asked us over the years.

There is, of course, a quite understandable fear that some powerful parents may wish to take over schools if too much encouragement is given to participate. In our experience, parents who are unaware of the dividing-line between professional expertise and legitimate customer interest form a tiny minority. Perhaps they are the same people who would try to tell a surgeon where to make the incision for their appendicitis operation. Although we occasionally hear horror stories from the United States about parents who select or veto set books or draw up the history syllabus, the real problem in Britain is not interference, but the many parents who still feel on the fringe of their children's education, only going into school for formal events or when there is a crisis. It is for them that this book is written, because they form the sensible, and often silent, majority.

A few years ago Patrick McGeeney, who did so much for home–school relationships and PTAs in the 1960s and 1970s, wrote a book which brought together the best of parental-involvement practices. He decided to call it *Parents are Welcome*. It is not a bad motto for schools.

Ted Wragg
John Partington

3

Chapter 1

PARENTS AND CHILDREN: RIGHTS AND RESPONSIBILITIES

Schools, politicians and parents

Over 90 per cent of the schools in England and Wales are run by the government. They are often referred to as 'state schools', although the correct term is 'maintained schools'. In practice, it is the local education authorities (LEAs) – counties such as Derbyshire, Gwent and Surrey, or cities such as Birmingham and Newcastle – which make many of the day-to-day decisions about matters such as how much money a particular school should be given.

Billions of pounds are spent by the government and millions by each of the hundred-plus LEAs on running the school system, so education itself becomes a party political matter, with the major political groups putting forward their ideas in their election manifesto. Elected members, local or national politicians, make vital decisions about education every year.

Politicians often take one of two positions about how education should be run. Some argue that, just as war is too important to be left to the generals, so education is too important to be left to parents and teachers. They believe that the elected politicians in LEAs and their professional officials should have the greatest say about the size and type of school in each area and where they should be built, which teachers should be appointed, or which schools children should attend.

The other view is that parents and teachers are in a much better position to see what children need and that more power should be given to each local community, particularly to the governing body of a school. This view predominated during the 1980s and major Education Acts passed in 1980, 1981, 1986 and 1988 gave parents, in particular, more powers and

4

opportunities to choose the schools they want for their children and to influence the way schools are run, though the 1988 Act also gave more power to the government as well.

The major rights given to parents in these four Acts are listed below:

1980 Act

1. The right to be elected by fellow parents on to school governing bodies.
2. The right to be given information about schools.
3. The right to be consulted over choice of school.
4. The right to see minutes of governors' meetings.

1981 Act

1. The right to a suitable education for a child with special educational needs.
2. The right to be consulted over the assessment of such needs.
3. The right to see documentation about a child's special educational needs.

1986 Act

1. The right to an annual meeting between parents and school governors.
2. The right to information about the school's financial affairs.
3. The right to appeal if a pupil is excluded from school for more than five days.

1988 Act

1. The right, with sufficient support from other parents, to bring about a ballot to decide whether the school should remain under local authority control.
2. The right to 'open enrolment' (stopping local education authorities from putting artificially low limits on schools to even out numbers across schools).

We now turn to a discussion of how these rights work in practice.

Finding out about schools

Schools and teachers develop good and bad reputations and these are sometimes difficult to correct even if they are wildly inaccurate. Similarly, parents want very different things for their children. Some parents look particularly for out-of-school activities, like sports or clubs or Continental journeys. Others will prefer schools which make impeccable behaviour inside and outside school their top priority, and other parents seek little beyond success in examinations.

Schools vary tremendously. A useful exercise for parents is to make a list of the things they want from school and then compare it with what is available – remembering, of course, that in an imperfect world they may well not get everything they would like.

To help parents to make an informed choice, the law requires all schools – not only fee-paying ones – to have information brochures which must be kept reasonably up to date. The law also lays down the minimum information about individual schools which must be included, but many LEAs provide additional information of interest to parents. There is some controversy over whether schools should, as the law requires, publish their examination results both in the national 'benchmark tests' at 7, 11 and 14, as well as in GCSE at 16. Teachers, particularly, fear that schools whose pupils are in general less able than those at other schools will be put at a disadvantage, even if the teaching of the less able is outstanding and achieves wonders.

School brochures can be obtained from each school. Parents are not limited to the nearest primary or secondary school, nor is there (within reason) any limit on how far away they can hunt for brochures (see 'Getting into a school' below). Some LEAs also place copies of all their school brochures in public libraries, or they can be obtained from the town hall. Do not be too influenced by an attractive, glossy printed brochure in comparison to simple photocopied sheets. The former might indicate a sincere desire by the school authorities to communicate well with prospective parents – or it might indicate a last desperate attempt to drum up pupils for a failing school.

Schools will usually be happy to give any further information needed and will arrange a visit for prospective parents. A very useful source of help and advice for parents is the Advisory Centre for Education (known usually as 'ACE') at 18 Victoria Park Square, London E2 9PB. As well as a bulletin every two months or so, ACE produces reports, pamphlets and books on all aspects of schools and education. There is a particularly useful booklet on parents' rights. We shall return to the question of choosing a school in Chapter 3.

Securing a place at a school

Between 1975 and 1985 the total number of pupils at primary schools fell from over five million to just under four. The estimate for 1991 is three million pupils in secondary schools as the decline of the population of primary schools works its way upwards.

This so-called 'problem of falling school rolls' has produced benefits for pupils and parents in that many if not most schools in the late 1980s and early 1990s have generally smaller classes and spare places to offer. This came about because the number of schools and teachers did not decline as fast as the birth-rate.

During the days of overcrowding of schools before the mid-1970s, it was commonplace for LEAs to 'zone' schools. This meant in practice that parents lived in the 'catchment areas' of local primary and secondary schools and were expected to send their children to these schools. It was always possible, however, for crafty and nimble-footed parents to avoid the local school if it did not, for some reason, meet their expectations and they understood how to play the system. 'Zoning' also benefited those families who could afford to move house to get the school of their choice, and many parents did in fact move. One well-known London estate agent frequently used the reputation of the local schools in his amusing advertising to push up the price of houses in the area.

At the time, the onus was on parents to show, if they wished, why their children should *not* go to the local school. Since the 1980 Education Act came into force, the onus is on LEAs to show why parents' choice of school should *not* be granted. The boot is on the other foot, as it were.

This does not mean, however, that LEAs cannot *suggest* a school for a child. They have a legal duty to ensure that sufficient school places are available for all children who need them and in carrying out that duty they obviously have to bear in mind where pupils are living. So LEAs will often write to parents saying that such and such a school is 'designated' (or some similar term) for their child. They might also suggest that if a pupil goes to Gasworks View County Primary School, he or she will be guaranteed a place at 11 at Ever Moaning Comprehensive nearby. But none of this amounts to compulsion by law and LEAs *must* make arrangements for all parents to express a preference for a particular school or schools.

LEAs must publish information about how to apply for places and often use the school brochures mentioned earlier to do so. Some schools are bound to be more sought after than others, and if a school has too many applicants for the places available, the so-called 'admission criteria' are used. These are bound to vary considerably from school to school. A Catholic school will obviously prefer Catholic pupils. Some schools may give preference to brothers and sisters of present and former pupils. If a school has some particular subject or subjects available which are unusual in the area, it may give special consideration to pupils with a particular interest or aptitude – such subjects may be, for example, classics or a third foreign language or music. There may be medical reasons (perhaps a child cannot travel very far) or a child may have a special educational need for which a school is particularly good at providing. A child meeting the conditions will usually be admitted.

Distance to school

If children under 8 live more than two miles from school or children between 8 and 16 live more than three miles from school, they are entitled to free travel to school. LEAs up and down the country carry out this obligation in many ways, from providing bus passes to special buses or even taxis.

The amount of public money spent in this way is not inconsiderable and LEAs hard-pressed for funds are sometimes driven to seeming absurdities, such as giving bus passes to the children who live on one side of a street, but not to those on the other. There are also apocryphal stories of mysterious men from 'the office' pushing around long poles with a wheel on the end in the dead of night trying to measure the exact distance from someone's front door to the school!

Children are at school for at least eleven years, so the amount of money spent by parents on school travel is often large. Not surprisingly, some have tried out some interesting theories. Is the distance to school to be measured from the front garden gate or from the front door? (Answer: the gate.) Is the length of the school drive included? (Answer: no.)

Money apart, a real concern of parents is the safety of their children who walk to school. The law is that children must take the 'nearest available route', provided, of course, that it is a public right of way! If parents think that the nearest available route is dangerous, they should accompany the child or if, say, the route is across a muddy field, they should buy suitable footwear. The point is that parents cannot choose a longer route for reasons that seem correct to them and thereby claim free school travel.

There are two possible exceptions to this. Since the passing of the 1986 Education Act, LEAs must 'have regard to' local difficulties in connection with the nearest available route and can, *if they choose*, make transport available. Similarly, LEAs can, *if they choose*, pay travelling costs to denominational schools which are further away than the nearest otherwise suitable school.

Failing to have one's choice

It would be impossible to guarantee that all parents and children could have their first choice of school. Sometimes the decisions about admissions made by school authorities cause feelings to run high and some parents are prepared to go to considerable lengths. During 1988, for example, some children in Dewsbury were kept away from school and educated privately by their parents for some months (see 'Education otherwise' on page 24) until a successful High Court battle forced the LEA to admit the children to the school the parents wanted them to attend.

Under the 1980 Education Act, a parent's choice of a particular school can be turned down by an LEA if:

1. the school is selective in some way (it may, for example, be a grammar school) and a pupil has not passed the entrance examination; or
2. there is some agreement between the LEA and the school governors which limits admissions: there may, perhaps, be an agreement that all the Anglican pupils in the area should go to that school; or
3. granting the parent's wish would 'prejudice the provision of efficient education or the efficient use of resources'.

Perhaps, inevitably, this last condition is vague and woolly and can be ripe ground for battle. It is impossible to catalogue the thousands of possibilities which might arise. A typical argument put forward by school governors, having reached their legal limit, might be that to admit any more pupils might make a popular teaching group too big and their school unit too large and less efficient.

The school is already full

Over the years this has been a great bone of contention between hopeful parents and school authorities, and it helps to try to see the problem from both sides.

A primary school known to the authors was built during the early 1960s and won a European architects' award for its design. It contained special areas set aside for crafts, music and a large library. It rapidly became very popular with parents.

During the early 1970s, when the number of children in the area was growing rapidly, the governors and headteacher yielded to pressure to admit more and more pupils. There was soon no alternative but to increase the staff and to use the specialist music, library and craft areas as normal classrooms. This meant, of course, that the pupils had less satisfactory opportunities in craft and music and the library was not available for use at all times as it should have been, because a class was being taught there.

The head, governors and parents were delighted at the prospect of shrinking numbers in the 1980s so that the school could again use the building as it had been designed. However, conscious that parental choice of schools was a 'hot' political issue, the government changed the law in 1988 so that schools are obliged to admit pupils up to the maximum numbers they admitted in 1979. For many schools, including the one described, that was the year in which the buildings had never been fuller! A school can be very successful and popular, but by over-crowding it to the legal limit it may soon become less successful and popular. Having one's way may backfire.

There is, incidentally, a procedure by which an appeal can be made to the Secretary of State to review the working of the limit in a particular school. If a good case is made out, the limit may be lowered.

Going to appeal

If parents are unsuccessful in gaining a place at the school they choose, their LEA should advise them that they can take their case before a local appeal panel specially set up for such matters.

Although these panels are set up by the LEAs, they do not merely rubber stamp decisions made elsewhere. The LEA appoints representatives on the panels but may not have a majority. Independent members, including the chair, can carry the day. Moreover, the panels are conducted under the Tribunals Act and follow a strict code of conduct. A parent who believes that a panel has conducted its business inefficiently or wrongly can, provided he or she can get the support of one local councillor, complain to the local government ombudsman. Quite a few have done so and had their complaints upheld. The complaint must be about what is called 'maladministration', though, not merely because the parent has not got his or her way!

There are two important points here. Firstly, it is up to the LEA to make its case against granting a parent's choice; it is not up to parents to show why their wishes should be granted. In the early days of these panels, after the 1980 Education Act, it was fairly common for the LEA representatives to say

11

to the panel simply: 'Sorry, but the school is full', and that was the end of the parents' appeal. However, a dispute about this in Glamorgan in 1983 went as far as the High Court. The judge argued that it could not have been the intention of Parliament, in setting up the appeals machinery, simply to have the panels listen to the same evidence and come to the same conclusions as the governors or LEA who had given the first refusal. They must have power to probe as far as they wished.

The effect of this ruling is that the LEA must *convince* the panel that the school is full, and not merely say so. The same judge said that, depending on the circumstances of the case, the only real expert on whether a particular class was full was the class teacher, not an education officer nor even perhaps the headteacher.

Another possibility from among many is that a parent's choice may be turned down at the first stage because the daily journey to and from school seems too long for a child of that age. The parents may, however, be able to convince an appeal panel that they can make suitable arrangements.

The second important point is that an appeal panel can, if it chooses, admit one or more pupils above any limit laid down for the school.

Children with special educaional needs

Parents have a duty under the law to see that their child is educated 'in accordance with any special educational needs he may have'. This, of course, can have a bearing on which school they choose for their child.

At one time children with physical handicaps or who experienced difficulties in learning at school were classified as 'educationally subnormal' or 'severely subnormal'. Most such children attended so-called 'special schools', run either by LEAs or by private associations specialising in such teaching.

The 1981 Education Act changed this significantly. The special definitions mentioned above have gone, and pupils in these categories are now referred to collectively as having 'special educational needs'. Moreover, within certain limits LEAs must try to ensure that these children are educated in ordinary schools (albeit, of course, with assistance) and not segregated.

The 1981 Act says that a child has a learning difficulty if:

1. he has a significantly greater difficulty in learning than the majority of children of his age; or
2. he has a disability which either prevents or hinders him from making use of educational facilities of a kind generally provided in schools, within the area of the local authority concerned, for children of his age; or
3. he is under the age of 5 and is, or would be if special educational provision were not made for him, likely to fall within the above paragraphs when over that age.

Children whose first language is not English (perhaps from immigrant families) are not included in the scope of the Act. Nor usually do LEAs include the needs of highly gifted and talented children, although it could be argued that they also have special educational needs.

LEAs now have a legal duty to find out which children in their schools have such needs and to take steps to provide for them as far as possible in ordinary schools. Having identified a child, the LEA must tell the parents that it is about to assess the child's needs and make a written statement of them. This process is most commonly known as 'statementing'. When a statement has been made, the LEA is under a legal duty to provide for it.

This might mean, in practice, that such parents' choice of school is limited to the ones which can help the child most because they have specially trained staff or different facilities – for example, a school might have to be a single-storey building so that a child in a wheelchair can gain access, or it may need to have books with large print for pupils who are partially sighted. Parents of children with special educational needs have the same rights of appeal as other parents, although Sir Keith Joseph as Secretary of State expressed the hope that such appeals would be few and far between since the LEA will have gone into the matter extremely carefully, and protracted haggling at appeals would probably not be in the child's best interests.

There have been arguments between parents and LEAs about the nature of provision for children with special educational needs. In one case a parent wished his child to be sent to a special school, whereas the authority preferred an ordinary school with special support provided. The difficulty was that independent advice recommended the special school. When the matter went to court, it was decided that LEAs are not under any legal obligation to provide a 'Utopian' system of education, as the judge put it. Their duty is to make suitable and adequate provision, even though it might be generally agreed that it might be better elsewhere.

Rights to consultation

Once their children are at school, parents sometimes feel that the family is in the grip of 'the system' and that their influence over it is less than they would like. This section is concerned with how far parents can and must by law be involved with decision-making about their childrens' schools.

The organisation of education

LEAs are elected political bodies which are charged by Parliament with running the education service in their areas. It is necessary to make this rather obvious statement because it is sometimes said that education should be non-political, the idea being presumably that professional experts should run it.

The difficulty with this idea is that it is based on the belief that professionals in the field of education would make better decisions than politicians, and would always agree among themselves. In practice, however, the issues which divide politicians divide experts in education as well.

Hence, the law takes the view that the ballot box is the place to argue out general education policy. For example, some parents in London in the late 1960s resented what they saw as the imposition of comprehensive schools in their area and took the argument as far as the High Court. They argued that they had not been consulted about the change. However, the court ruled that the views of the then controlling political party had been clear at the time of the local government elections and that the only recourse in law for the complainers was to vote the local authority out next time round. Similarly, the courts upheld the right of an LEA after a local election in Tameside in the 1970s to go back on a decision of its political opponents, now in opposition, to 'go comprehensive'. Nowadays the issues are likely to be school closures due to falling pupil rolls and the reorganisation of education for 16 to 19-year-olds.

A distinction needs to be made here. As we stated earlier, parents *must* be consulted about the education of their own children when they are asked to choose a school. Collective consultation is a matter for the ballot box: there is no legal obligation for an LEA to consult any local group.

This does not mean that LEAs can do whatever they like. The Secretary of State has power under the 1944 Education Act to stop LEAs if they act or are proposing to act 'unreasonably'. Secretaries of State for Education and Science from all political parties have used this power or threatened to use it (which is usually enough) when parents and others have complained to them. They have stopped unreasonable school reorganisation in Wales, stopped one LEA from enforcing a union 'closed shop' in Durham and prevented another from continuing to take disciplinary action against a headteacher after enquiries had shown that she had little or no case to answer. In one celebrated case, parents of children in the little village of Burlescombe, supported by the governors, persuaded the Secretary of State to stop the Devon LEA from imposing a redeployed teacher on their school against their wishes.

Many parents see things differently from the courts. Education is only one of many issues about which they vote in local elections and only very rarely is it high on the list of issues at the hustings. The reality, perhaps, for most parents, is that rightly or wrongly they rarely seek out education issues at local elections and the legal position seems irrelevant.

The position of parents *vis-à-vis* 'the system' is changing, however.

In 1985, a judge ruled in a case about school reorganisation in the London Borough of Brent that parents had a legitimate expectation, but no actual legal right, to be consulted fully. It

15

was not sufficient for the LEA merely to say what it was going to do and then to do it.

Parents in Bristol succeeded in stopping a reorganisation plan which would have had the effect of reducing the number of places at single-sex boys' schools to below the numbers available at single-sex girls' schools. The court agreed that this was a breach of the Sex Discrimination Act. Moreover, the courts will always side with parents and others affected if LEAs do not scrupulously observe the procedures laid down by Parliament for the reorganisation of schools. They have more than once defended individual parents' rights and caused enormous local chaos in doing so.

A new power from the European Convention on Human Rights, enforced through the European Court of Human Rights, is becoming available for parents. The British Government signed this treaty and, although it is not yet formally part of our law, Parliament has reacted positively to it in a number of ways. Perhaps the best known of these was the abolition of corporal punishment in schools by the 1986 Education Act. Under the European Convention, the government must respect the right of parents to hold 'religious or philosophical convictions' about their children's education and seek within reason to satisfy them. The 1988 Education Reform Act responded to this to a degree by increasing the control of schools by parents and the local community and significantly reducing the power of LEAs to determine any overall policy for all schools in their area.

Consultation through the governors' annual general meeting

Since the 1986 Education Act came into force, school governors are required to hold an annual meeting with parents of children at the school. This is intended as a major process of consultation.

Governors of schools had hitherto been a rather shadowy lot in most parents' experience, occasionally turning up at prize-giving ceremonies and the like. Beyond that, most parents knew that they existed but did not know what they did.

Governors nowadays have considerable power, and it is right that they should be accountable to their clients. They control the school's budget, hire and fire teachers and most other staff, and keep an eye on the curriculum and disciplinary policy of the school.

The annual governors' meeting with parents provides an opportunity to get to grips with those who can influence matters. To begin with, many governors decided that their new high-profile existence was a little too stressful and resigned. Some governing bodies were astonished to receive resignations from people they had not been aware of until then.

By law, parents and all employees at the school must receive an agenda and papers for the meeting at least two weeks in advance. The governors' report to the parents (the thick document in the middle!) should be comprehensive enough to inform them about life in the school during that year. If it is not, the parents can try to have a resolution passed prescribing the sort of information they want next year. If the demand warrants it, the law supports you in asking for a report in another language – for example Welsh or Punjabi. The law is specific about the content of the report. It must state that the management of the school by the headteacher and the governors is up for discussion. It must give the names of all the governors and who appointed them, as well as providing the names and addresses of the chairperson and clerk so that you can contact them. It must explain next year's arrangement for the election of parent-governors. It must also supply a summary of the school budget for the preceding year and state what measures have been taken to strengthen links with the community, including the police.

Parents may ask anything they like at the meeting, although it is generally accepted that any matter affecting individual teachers and parents is best dealt with privately. (Sounding off at length about Dr Boreham's French teaching might land you with a slander writ unless you really know what you are talking about. It is not a defence to say that you actually believed what young Wilberforce told you. . . .)

Anyone in the audience feeling frisky can ask the chairman of governors (he/she will be sitting in the middle of the front row) whether the governors or the head wrote the report. If it turns out that the head wrote it, the question ought to be asked how it can be called a '*Governors*' Report to Parents'? It is not, of course, because the governors cannot write; is it perhaps because they do not really know what has been happening in their school? When are the next elections for governors? Most annual meetings are peaceful affairs, but it is the one public occasion when parents dissatisfied with the school can make their point.

The meeting can pass resolutions in the usual way. These are not binding on the school, *but* at the next annual meeting parents are entitled to hear what became of their collective advice and why, if so, it has not been acted upon. There should be an item on the agenda next year to this effect. It is a legal requirement.

Becoming a parent-governor

Any parent who has a child at a maintained school is entitled to stand as a parent-governor. Elections are held regularly and governors serve for four years and can be re-elected. Schools have from two to five parent-governors.

The largest single group on governing bodies nowadays is the group of co-opted members, chosen for the contribution they can make to the school. The law requires the business community to be represented in this group, but it does not define exactly what this means. A parent can also be co-opted as a governor, but obviously for his or her expertise in some helpful field rather than expertise in producing offspring.

Governing bodies, as constituted nowadays, are markedly different from the time when they were dominated by LEA nominees – often overwhelmingly also by one or other political party. Some highly political authorities have resented this change and some politicians have sought to strengthen their party's control by nobbling parent and co-opted governors or seeking to have their supporters elected.

The most important characteristic of a good parent-governor is a sincere interest in the school and a sensitivity to what other parents would like. Being an active party member comes much further down the list of priorities.

Governors' meetings are held at least once a term and there is always the prospect of public scrutiny at the annual governors' meetings to look forward to. Many LEAs provide initial training for governors and the local library has plenty of material on what the job entails. In effect, anything to do with the school can be raised at governors' meetings and nowadays most important decisions are made there.

It is worth noting that parent-governors are not delegates; they are not sent along to sing a predetermined song. They are elected in their own right as representative parents and can quite legitimately support something at meetings which they know will not please some of their supporters. We return to the question of parent-governors in Chapter 4.

Parents and independent schools

Although this book is written primarily for parents with children in maintained schools, it is worth remembering that about 10 per cent of parents send their children to different types of school.

Although the terms 'independent' or 'private' school are most widely used, the official designation is 'non-maintained' school. The point is that these schools are not maintained by LEAs, but in some other way, usually through fees. Instead of paying for education exclusively through taxes, parents of children at these schools also pay fees directly to the school.

The existence of these schools has troubled government from time to time and provokes sharp disagreement. However, they have survived four major government commissions of inquiry (some of them clearly intent on their abolition!) during and since the nineteenth century and their existence seems assured for the foreseeable future at least. The term 'independent' school usually conjures up in most people's minds the major public boarding-schools such as Winchester, Eton or Harrow. However, nowadays, the City Technology Colleges are also 'independent' schools, as are to some extent the 'grant-maintained' or 'opted-out' schools created by the 1988 Act.

When parents send their children to non-maintained schools, they enter into an agreement which may depend largely on what they want for their child and the characteristics of the individual school. In many cases, the entire slant of the curriculum may be peculiar to the school: the teaching may perhaps be of a religious denomination, such as Moravian, Muslim or Jewish. The way the school is conducted may also be unusual: a good example here is Summerhill, the world-renowed boarding-school founded by A. S. Neill at Leiston in Suffolk, where there is an emphasis on self-determination and treating pupils as children rather than as mini-adults. There are also schools which specialise in the education of children with particular learning difficulties, such as dyslexia. Others may have expertise in teaching autistic children.

Parents with children at these schools have fewer statutory rights than parents with children at maintained schools. There are difficulties over parents being governors, for example, because parents are beneficiaries of the school, and it would be improper for a parent who is paying fees to be a member of a body which decides on the level of those fees. Also, because parents usually live a long way from boarding-schools, close consultation and meetings with governors is impracticable.

Nevertheless, parents' rights are substantial. If they are unhappy with what they get, parents can always move their children to another school. The agreement signed with most schools will be that pupils will be moved only at the end of a term, so there may be some liability for fees if a pupil is moved at any other time.

At the moment, the ban on corporal punishment does not extend under British law to non-maintained schools. However, the rights of pupils as regards 'inhuman and degrading treatment' under the European Convention extends to *all* schools, not only the maintained ones. The demise of corporal punishment everywhere is now a distinct possibility.

The most common major causes of friction between parents and non-maintained schools have been exclusion from school and punishment. Where a pupil has been excluded, parents can allege that in law the school has broken the contract to educate, and try to have the fees for the period when their child was kept out of school reimbursed. Generally speaking, however, the courts have always upheld the right of head-teachers of non-maintained schools to exclude pupils on 'reasonable' grounds, just as they have the right of headteachers of maintained schools. The essential difference is that the agreement between parents and non-maintained schools may well contain implicit as well as explicit features which are binding, particularly where behaviour is concerned. Put crudely, it may mean that types of behaviour by pupils which *might* go unremarked by headteachers and governors in maintained schools might provoke sharp reaction in non-maintained schools. The courts would be unlikely to object to this, unless, of course, some major issue of principle were involved.

This said, it is worth remembering that the legal precedents in areas such as school rules, accidents to pupils, the authority of school rules and punishments – most of which are valid today in maintained schools – were for the most part established in the public schools of the late nineteenth century, when the government system of education was in its infancy. It is noteworthy, too, how much of the terminology of modern comprehensive schools derives from the non-maintained schools, which in their time devised school 'houses', 'housemasters', 'pastoral care' and 'prefects'.

Children's rights

This chapter has been about parents' rights. However, many lawyers and educationalists are increasingly interested in the proposition that children should have rights of their own in education and not, as the law presently stands, be legal chattels as it were and the responsibility of their parents. Interest has grown to the point at which, as a contribution to the International Year of the Child, the British Government in 1979 set up the Children's Legal Centre (20 Compton Terrace, London N1 2UN).

Take wrongful exclusion from school for example. This happens occasionally and, if the parent appeals as the 1986 Education Act allows, the governors usually recognise the error and the pupil returns to school. But what if the parents cannot be bothered to appeal? Or, worse, are rather glad that their son is excluded because he can now take on a job? The pupil himself has no right of appeal under the law and has been wrongfully deprived of his schooling.

Pupils can also be subjected to their parents' convictions about education, regardless of whether they think them correct or barmy. In the final analysis, it is the parents who are consulted by law about schools and curriculum, not the pupils.

Similarly, as we noted earlier, the law presently tends to turn a blind eye to parents' failings in the education of their children, provided that the children attend school regularly. That parents, for example, do not check homework or emphasise good behaviour is ignored by the law, despite the fact that parents must 'cause their child to be educated'.

The European Convention on Human Rights is particularly of interest here. Although it was conceived in the period after the Second World War and was intended to ensure that the destruction of civil liberties during the Nazi era would never be repeated, its wording makes it applicable to education systems. Although most sections begin with the words 'No-one shall . . .', 'Everyone shall . . .' or 'All persons shall . . .', no distinction is made between adults and children.

As we have mentioned already, the distinct likelihood that corporal punishment in British schools would be seen under the European Convention as 'inhuman or degrading treatment or punishment' (Article 3) was a major pressure leading to its abolition in 1986. The abolition does not extend to independent schools but the threat of 'appealing to Strasbourg' (the home of the European Court) would stop such schools in their tracks. It is thought-provoking to those interested in children's rights that parents can, if they choose, pay fees to ensure that their children are beaten as schools see fit – and the children have no say in the matter!

Several other articles in the Convention have a bearing on the way children are treated at school. Article 8 states that 'Everyone has the right to respect for his private and family life, his home and his correspondence', which implies that compulsory searches of children if property is missing (this might also be assault under present law) or interference with their private mail (for example, in boarding-schools) are breaches of the Convention. Similarly, according to Article 10: 'Everyone has the right to freedom of expression. This right shall include freedom to hold opinions and to receive and impart information without interference. . . .' Article 11 talks of the 'right of peaceful assembly'. It seems, therefore, that pupils have the right to their own meetings and to their own notice-boards and the like in school.

Perhaps most interestingly of all, the Convention states that 'No person shall be denied the right to education'. However, the same section goes on to qualify this by reference to parents' rights mentioned earlier.

Chapter 2

PARENTS AND THE LAW OF EDUCATION

In Britain, education between 5 and 16 is compulsory. Schooling is not.

This, perhaps surprising, distinction is contained in the 1944 Education Act. It says that parents must 'cause their children to receive ... education either by ... attendance at school or otherwise'. 'Otherwise' can mean that parents themselves teach their children or get others to do it.

It is difficult to find out just how many parents take this route, although it is clear that the numbers are growing. Many such parents are themselves professional teachers, something which is in itself food for thought. There is now a national organisation, Education Otherwise, which helps parents who are educating their children at home, particularly with the legal snags they sometimes encounter.

Home education has also been used by parents in the past as a kind of protest against an LEA's refusal to admit their children to the school they wanted. But calling it a protest does not relieve parents of the duty to educate while the children are not at school.

Parents are obliged to ensure that the education of their children is 'efficient'. This term has never been defined. In fact, LEAs, whose job it is to ensure that parents carry out their duty to educate, rarely if ever do more than insist on regular *attendance* at school.

This is decidedly unfair on parents who educate at home. They are often called upon to demonstrate to LEAs and sometimes in court just what their children are learning at home. If, on the other hand, a child attends school regularly but learns nothing, the LEA takes no action at all against the parent! There is the famous story of the magistrates who, over twenty years ago, were hearing a case against a mother who was educating her children at home. The LEA alleged that the education was not 'efficient'. The magistrates asked the children general knowledge questions in court and decided against the mother when one of the children told them (among other things, of course) that a camel's hump contains fat. There were red faces on the bench when the child later turned out to be right. It is also some cause for concern that in these cases parents are presumed guilty until they prove themselves innocent – something highly unusual in law.

It is often difficult for LEAs to agree that what a particular parent is doing in the way of education may be superior to what is on offer in their own schools. Too often they try to get these parents to reproduce at home what the schools in the area offer – but that is often why the parents did not send their children there in the first place.

The law takes the education of children very seriously and prescribes fines and prison for parents who fail to educate. Children may also be taken into local authority care to ensure their education, even if their homes and parents are in all other respects excellent.

Regular attendance

If parents choose to educate their children by sending them to school, as most do, they must send them 'regularly', to quote the 1944 Education Act. This means attendance for the whole time a school is open, usually ten half-day sessions per week during term-time.

The law does not allow parents to 'mix it' and educate partly in school and partly away. On reflection, it will be seen that the law cannot really take any other view, since chaos would arise in most schools and LEAs would be spending most of their time chasing around to see whether Wayne, Esmeralda, Duane and Winston really were being 'educated otherwise' last Friday afternoon.

Headteachers use their common sense over this. If, from time to time, parents have something in mind which might be of better value than what the school has on offer, the head might agree to a day's absence – but it remains technically a breach of the law.

Parents, and sometimes teachers and headteachers are frequently unaware that unpunctuality is also illegal. A child who persistently turns up late for school is not attending 'regularly' as required, and the parent can be prosecuted. It is worth knowing too that 'failure to attend regularly' is what lawyers call an 'absolute offence'. *Why* a child turns up late or is absent for an unlawful reason (see below) is not admissible as evidence in court: if he or she is late or absent, an offence has been committed – end of argument. Of course, if an LEA is sympathetic to the reason, it might just decide not to prosecute in the first place.

The same applies if a parent genuinely does not know that Jeremy has been 'bunking off' instead of going to school, something which happens frequently. An offence has still been committed. The implication here – as was mentioned above in the section on free transport to school – is that Jeremy's parents should escort him to school by the left ear if they wish to avoid a fine. The point, once again, is that the law requires parents to 'cause their child to receive . . . education', which is more than merely waving goodbye every morning at the front door.

Illness may also legitimately keep a child off school, but it must be the child's illness, not someone else's. It used to be common for older children, particularly girls, to stay at home to look after sick relatives. This is now against the law. Similarly, children are entitled to days off for religious observances of the Church to which their parents belong. This too was sometimes abused, and crafty parents tried to justify their children's absences by claiming that they were Anglican on a Monday, Catholic on Friday and so on, depending on whether the day of absence was a saint's day. LEAs now ask parents to declare a child's religion in advance!

Parents and the curriculum

When parents choose a school, they choose a curriculum. School brochures should give sufficient information to parents about the way in which the National Curriculum is interpreted in each school, particularly where secondary schools are concerned. Primary schools have traditionally a rather more flexible curriculum, although the headteacher will be able to give fuller information on any points of concern.

Parents have a right to see that the curriculum, as described, is implemented, although circumstances might make it virtually impossible to guarantee it. If a primary school, for whatever reason, loses the only teacher who can give guitar lessons and a replacement is not available, there is little that can be done. Incidentally, a school is fully entitled to include details of its clubs and other extra-curricular activities in its brochure if it wishes, but these are voluntary activities by the teachers and they cannot be forced to undertake them. During the period of the teachers' industrial action in the early 1980s, it rankled with many teachers that parents complained bitterly that they were unwilling to take on extra, unpaid school clubs and other activities.

Secondary schools usually offer various subject choices, although schools with smaller staffs have more limited choice. Usually schools will do their best to comply with parents' requests, but sometimes there are limitations. It is common practice, for example, to put subjects into groups and let pupils choose a group. Since the timetables are different for each group, it is virtually impossible for a pupil to 'pick and mix' among the groups. Parents who ask for this are really requesting an individual timetable for their child.

School rules

Schools clearly need basic rules for all their pupils in order to run smoothly. Parents also have rules for their own children.

This analogy is important because teachers in Britain are looked upon as parents by the law. The law also recognises that, just as parents can disagree with each other about how their offspring should be treated, so teachers and parents can legitimately have different ideas. The point is that teachers are not in the position of having to take orders from parents because they too, as it were, have an equal voice.

It surprises many people to hear that school rules are technically part of the law of the land. Education Acts have laid down that every school shall have 'Articles of Government' and, among many other things, these contain the statement that the headteacher shall look after the 'internal discipline, management and control' of the school. Since the 1986 Education Act, the law has required the headteacher – who is also a governor ex officio – to 'have regard to' any policy on discipline laid down by the school governors.

If parents find themselves at odds with a school rule, an approach to the headteacher is the first possibility. Some parents have in the past gone 'over the top' in creating a fuss at schools (even if fully justified), so much so that Parliament saw fit in 1982 to make 'causing a nuisance on educational premises' a specific criminal offence. (Fine: £50 for those who might remain undeterred!)

If that fails, an approach to the governors might work. This could be via one of the parent-governors or to the chairman of the governors whose name and address ought to be displayed fairly prominently near the entrance to the school. If it is not, parents can bring the matter up at the annual governors' meeting with parents.

There is, of course, no guarantee that any rule will be changed as a result of parental pressure. And it is most unlikely that the school will agree to exempting one or two pupils from it. What parents should *not* do is to encourage their child to break or to ignore the rule, as this is a sure way to disaster. This point was made in the 1950s when school uniform was much more common than it is today. A parent in Warrington insisted on sending his daughter to school in slacks rather than the regulation skirt. After a warning period, the head refused the pupil admission each day. The LEA prosecuted the parent for failure to cause the child to attend regularly.

The parent argued that the child *had* attended school: the headteacher had locked her out. The court held, however, that the duty of a parent is to 'cause to receive . . . education', so that sending his daughter to school knowing that she would not be admitted was a breach of the duty of the parent under the law.

School rules must, however, be *reasonable*: a decision to

admit only red-headed children, for example, would not be. It is doubtful, too, whether school uniform would stand up nowadays as an enforceable rule. Legislation about sex and racial discrimination also applies. There cannot be any rule saying, for example, that only boys may study engineering or girls domestic science. And the courts have held that to order a Sikh boy to remove his turban in favour of school uniform is a breach of race relations legislation.

Homework

In general terms, the law takes the view that by choosing a school a parent accepts the rules of that school. If one joins any club, one accepts the rules.

Homework may be a rule of the school. If so, the policy will probably be made clear in the brochure. It is not clear, however, whether it is legally enforceable to the point at which a child may be punished for failure to do it. The only legal action fought over homework was as long ago as 1884 and the facts of the case were so special that it is not a good guide. In that case, it was held that detention after school hours for poorly done homework was unlawful.

Punishments

A school's policy on discipline should be outlined in its brochure and parents have a right to expect that the school will adhere to it. Unusual forms of punishment have always been frowned upon by the courts, but the position since the 1980 Education Act is that parents have a right to know the sort of sanctions which will be meted out if their child deserves it.

Corporal punishment was outlawed by Parliament (by one vote) in the 1986 Education Act. It is not easy to define and many LEAs see it as much wider in meaning than the slipper or cane administered by the headteacher. In some parts of the country, it is being interpreted as virtually any physical contact with children.

Teachers may, however, legally use physical force to prevent injury to children – for example, to prevent Algernon and Jeremy from fighting tooth and nail in the playground every lunchtime.

29

Teachers who break the law in this respect are liable to be dismissed. Parents can also take legal action for assault.

Parents cannot authorise a school or a teacher to use corporal punishment on their children, although it is surprising how many parents suggest this when it seems that their child is about to be excluded from school for some serious misdemeanour. Teachers cannot plead parental support if they punish in this way and are disciplined.

Detention after school

Detention after school against the parent's express wishes is unlawful and at worst is something akin to kidnapping! For this reason, schools which have a detention system − not all do − usually send a note home to say that Darren will be expected to do his penance between say 4 and 4.30 of a Wednesday afternoon, and ask for a parental signature of agreement. This is particularly important, of course, where special transport arrangements might be needed. Some schools have a detention system at lunchtime for this reason.

Even so, such an agreement does not really amount to a binding contract and a parent may withdraw permission, which the school *must* respect. That said, however, there seems little point in choosing a school for its merits and then trying to act against it!

Teachers' responsibility for children

Teachers are regarded under British law as additional parents to the children for whom they are responsible. Teachers are not only instructors in the subjects on the school timetable: they have a general responsibility for the whole child as a human being. This is why so many teachers give up their time for out-of-school activities such as clubs and sports teams. The situation is markedly different in mainland Europe, where teachers are seen more as Civil Servants with a role limited to instruction.

When it comes to preventing harm to children, British teachers are judged by the standard of the careful and prudent parent. But the courts of law recognise that careful and prudent parents do not produce twenty-odd children and more −

the sort of number with which teachers have to deal daily! However, teachers *are* expected to have an expert knowledge of what their charges are likely to get up to, but here again the courts recognise that teachers are not equipped with a crystal ball. Pupils are able to injure themselves in the most surprising ways.

Parents are sometimes able to persuade the courts or school authorities that teachers have been negligent towards their child, as the law puts it. However, all accident cases are different from each other and, apart from the general principles outlined above, decisions on whether an injured child should receive some compensation depend on the facts of each case. It is certainly *not* the case that, if a child suffers an injury at school, someone must be responsible. Children are injured at home too, and if every parent were to be held responsible in law for every injury suffered by a child in their care, it is likely that breeding would go out of fashion even more than it already has. The important test is whether the parent can show that the teacher could reasonably have foreseen the accident and prevented it.

It is also worth bearing in mind that because a parent and a teacher or a school disagree about whether a particular activity in school is foreseeably dangerous, it does not always follow that the parent must be right. Parents have taken legal action over the years following injuries to children playing leap-frog in the school playground or making slides on frost and ice in winter. The courts have held that these are traditional children's activities, both in and outside school, even if individual parents ban them for their own children. Parents can, of course, dissuade their children from taking part in these playground activities or choose another school.

Negligent teaching

There have been hardly any cases of parents suing because their children have been negligently taught, although American experience suggests that it might be on the way. If a pupil is perhaps wrongly not entered for an examination, or entered for the wrong one, or is perhaps given the wrong set books to study – all things which happen not infrequently –

there is seemingly a case to answer. In 1966 students in Kent were successful in suing over poor marking of their examination scripts.

Parents' liability for their children

Just as schools may be liable to parents for wrongs, so may parents be liable to society.

The 1982 Criminal Justice Act made it possible for the courts to make parents pay for damage committed by their children or any fines imposed. Parents themselves are not held responsible for their children's actions, only for any monetary consequences.

Thus, if a pupil throws a stone through a window on his way home from school and the magistrates decide that it was not accidental, the parent is liable to pay fines and compensation.

Local authorities, too, can be held responsible like parents. There have been cases where children in the care of a local authority have committed acts of vandalism, such as ripping the seats of hired coaches to football matches, and the authority has paid compensation. Similarly, an LEA can be held to be negligent. In one case, a young child was allowed to dash out of a school yard and into a road, causing a lorry driver to swerve and hit a telegraph pole. The driver's widow successfully sued the LEA for substantial compensation.

School costs

As with the National Health Service, education is not entirely free. Maintained ('State') schools may not charge fees, but there is an increasing tendency to charge for extra-curricular activities. Each LEA has a policy on this.

Parents are not charged for activities which are an inescapable part of an examination course, such as the National Curriculum, although the LEA has the final say on which examinations are covered by this. So, for example, a child who learns a musical instrument as part of an approved course will not be charged for tuition. Individual tuition may otherwise be charged, even if it takes place during the school day.

Because the lunch-break is now seen as falling outside the

school day, parents may also be charged if they wish their children to take part in school clubs at that time.

Parents may also have to contribute to the cost of school journeys if more than half the time spent on the journey falls outside school hours.

Examinations

Since public examinations form an important part of school courses, the entry fees for the examinations are paid by the school. However, if a pupil who has been entered fails to turn up, parents are liable to pay the fees wasted.

A school is not obliged to enter a pupil for a public examination if there appears to be little chance of success. The GCSE at 16+ *may* be an exception to this, since the intention behind the examination is that even the weakest pupils should attain at least the lowest grades. Parents can, of course, volunteer to pay the entrance fee if they are unhappy with the school's judgement. If the parents are proved right, the school may reimburse them.

Apart from this, parents can enter their children for any examination as 'private candidates'. This is done by contacting the examining authority directly.

LEAs can take parents to court if they fail to pay any money they owe the school.

Exclusion from school

Exclusion is the term used since the 1986 Education Act to describe what most of us remember as expulsion or suspension. It can be temporary or permanent.

Nobody lightly denies a child 'the right to education' as the European Convention on Human Rights puts it, and the procedures for excluding pupils are rightly very thorough. Only the headteacher of a school can start the process and in many cases headteachers come under great pressure from their colleagues to do so, sometimes against the headteacher's better instincts. All teachers involved in exclusion proceedings recognise that it is an admission of failure on their part, but there comes a time when a pupil has pushed his luck too far and the best interests of his classmates come first.

When a child is excluded, a note is sent home. A headteacher can suspend for up to five days on his or her own authority, but beyond that parents must be told that they can appeal to the governors. In these proceedings, the headteacher, although probably a governor, is only a witness who explains why in his or her view the exclusion was necessary. Governors have a duty to look at the matter dispassionately, although some do need reminding that automatically siding with the headteacher as a fellow governor is wrong, as is the knee-jerk reaction of some governors with a trade union background to side with whatever the teachers' union may have to say about the pupil.

If a pupil is permanently excluded, the matter has to go to the LEA, where it will be looked at again. When this happened in Manchester in 1985, in the case of a group of boys who scrawled graffiti on a school wall, there was a prolonged battle between the teachers who wanted them out and the LEA which wanted them back at school. The 1986 Education Act gave LEAs the power to *order* reinstatement of excluded pupils – a power which they had hitherto not had. And just to show that justice was being done on all sides, the same Act gave governors the opportunity to appeal to the LEA against reinstatement. All this could take months, while the pupil and his parents wonder what on earth is going on. However, if they have any sense, they will have found another school.

'Opting out'

This is the term popularly used to describe a process introduced by the 1988 Education Reform Act. It means that, in principle, if constructive relationships between a school and its local authority have broken down, a school may decide to go its own way. Incidentally, the right is limited to schools with more than 300 pupils.

If a school decides to sever most of its links with the local authority, it becomes financed directly from the Department of Education and Science – the level of finance being roughly what the school had received before opting out. It also acquires the new title of 'grant-maintained' school.

A secret postal ballot of parents must be conducted by the

governors. Although it is most likely to be the governors who start the process of opting out, parents have the right under the 1988 Act to petition the governors to do so.

The law requires the full implications of the move to be spelt out to parents before the ballot. At least 50 per cent of parents must vote for the ballot to be valid. It is interesting that at the time of writing some 40 ballots have been held and the average turnout of parents to vote has been between 80 and 90 per cent. A school cannot, for example, opt out in order to change its character; it cannot decide to change from being a comprehensive school to being a grammar school, or from single-sex to co-educational. That sort of change requires a quite separate set of administrative procedures.

Being a governor of a grant-maintained school is also likely to be a much more onerous job, since more of the day-to-day decision-making of the school is likely to come with the change. Of course, many governors will be keen to grasp the challenge.

'Opting out' also requires the consent of the Secretary of State after the ballot. Normally, of course, it would be given, but there might be circumstances in which, although the proper procedures had been adhered to, there might still be doubt about going ahead. A low response in the ballot might persuade the Secretary of State to hold things up, or perhaps even a massive response with a majority of only one.

Chapter 3

HOW SCHOOLS WORK

For those who do not spend most of their weekdays in school, it can seem a very confusing and complex institution. It is not unlike an intelligent Martian arriving in the middle of a game of cricket. Everyone else appears to know what the rules are, where to run or walk, what to wear, the purpose of the game and what the roles of the various participants are, but the Martian is bewildered by much of what he sees.

Although there are many similarities between schools, no two are exactly alike. What distinguishes one school from another is the uniqueness of key people, like the head and teachers, and the differences in catchment areas, pupils and their families, buildings and traditions. There are some schools with modern attractive buildings, high-calibre staff, well-motivated pupils and excellent facilities, and others, even in the same town, with the exact opposite of all these. Even schools which appear, on the surface, to be similar, might have quite different forms of organisation or classroom atmosphere.

Parents are thus in a difficult position. On the one hand they are the guardians of their children; on the other, they have given over for several hours each day a significant amount of their responsibility to teachers who are legally acting on their behalf – *in loco parentis*. It is important, therefore, for parents to understand how schools actually work. Much of the friction that occurs from time to time between parents and schools is the result of one party not understanding how the other functions.

Teachers need to appreciate that many parents feel apprehensive when they come into a school. Some may have unhappy memories of an unpleasant childhood when authoritarian teachers intimidated them. Others may not be at ease in a professional environment, unhappy about picking up the phone to make an appointment, writing a letter to convey information, or simply unsure, when arriving at the school gate, where to go or whom to see. What is obvious and taken for granted by the insider – where the school office is, what the deputy head looks like, or where staff congregate at break-time – is a complete mystery to most parents making an occasional visit.

Buildings themselves can be forbidding. Some are warm and reassuring to the visitor, often having a clear sign prominently displayed welcoming visitors, sometimes in more than one language, and explaining that anyone visiting the school should go to the school office, with directions on how to get there. There may be a reception area right by the main entrance with a window labelled 'enquiries' and a friendly school secretary who puts people at their ease. Equally, there may be no obvious main entrance and the school office may be on the second floor at the top of a rear staircase, or there may be several different buildings on the same site with no signposts and no labels. The feeling for a visiting parent is not unlike driving through Birmingham for the first time, terrified you will take the wrong exit.

This two-way obligation is especially important at a time of rapid change in education. In the light of the many developments in children's opportunities, curriculum, examinations, the management of schools and the responsibilities of teachers and governors which are fully described in other books in this 'Education Matters' series, it is crucial that schools keep parents well informed, but it is also vital that parents brief themselves.

The structure of the school

Although schools can be quite different from each other, they also have certain similarities. In order to discharge their responsibilities, they have to organise themselves with a high degree of efficiency, otherwise, especially in large secondary schools, children would be a mere number instead of the unique individual their parents know they are.

Primary schools tend to be organised on less formal lines than secondary schools simply because they are smaller and because each class is usually taught substantially by one teacher rather than the ten or so different ones who might teach a secondary class. A large primary school would count as quite a small secondary school, and in most local authorities there are about five or six times as many primary as secondary schools. In a rural county, there might be some 300 or 400 primary schools and nearly half of these could be small village schools with two, three or four teachers and 100 or fewer pupils.

Even in very small schools, however, there must be some degree of organisation to ensure that the curriculum is properly covered, visits and field-trips arranged, dinner money collected and finances and resources managed effectively. Therefore, primary schools have a headteacher, usually a deputy and then a few teachers who hold posts with special responsibility, perhaps for the science, maths or music in the school, or who look after the library and other learning resources.

During the last few years there has been considerable pressure on primary schools to engage in more specialist teaching. When surveys by Her Majesty's Inspectorate (HMI) showed that science, in particular, was not being taught well, with few teachers feeling confident in their handling of physical science topics, such as magnetism and electricity or microelectronics, a number of schools appointed a teacher specifically to act as science co-ordinator. The pattern in many schools nowadays, therefore, is to keep to the format of allowing one teacher to teach one class for most of the week, but to encourage some to become specialist co-ordinators in fields like music, maths or science, and to take classes other than their own in their specialised field. Without adopting wholesale the fully specialist model of teaching current in most secondary schools, primary schools have encouraged the development of the semi-specialist.

The primary child's day is usually organised around blocks of time set aside for different aspects of the National Curriculum, such as number, language, music, science, physical education and so on. In addition to these subjects, however, there are a whole series of topics and projects, some personal to the individual, others pursued by the whole class. A child might be taking part in a class project on 'Fairgrounds', stimulated by the popular BBC schools television programme 'Watch', but might be pursuing an individual project on 'Otters' because this was a personal interest.

The more intimate atmosphere of the smaller primary school cannot be replicated in a large secondary school, but most schools have made great efforts to operate in such a way that children can develop a sense of belonging. The principal unit is often the subject department, but in order to cater for what schools call 'pastoral care', there is a structure which cuts across all departments. This can be a little confusing for parents, because if their child has a problem in maths they may find that it is brought to their attention by a 'form tutor' or 'year group head', as well as by the maths teacher concerned.

This is because the organisation in many schools looks like a crossword-puzzle shape. In the columns going down are the various subjects, such as maths, science, English and so on, but in the rows going across there are the heads of each year, like the first, second, or sometimes heads of upper, middle or lower school. Their job is to look at each child's achievement across all subjects and link with each class tutor who does the same for the 30 or so pupils in his or her care. If this did not happen, then children would only be seen as the sum of their achievements in several subjects, rather than as a complete individual.

The structure of the whole secondary school reflects this same concern. The head is usually assisted by more than one deputy, and it is often the deputies who each take front-line responsibility for such matters as curriculum, pastoral care or relationships with parents and the community. Many schools have a sort of senior teachers' 'Cabinet', consisting of the head, deputies, heads of year-group and heads of subject departments, perhaps with a smaller senior management team which includes the head, deputies and one or two senior teachers. Parents wanting to discuss their child's progress might meet a subject teacher, a head of year-group, a form tutor or a deputy head, depending whether the focus of the discussion was on one particular subject, the whole curriculum or their child's general behaviour in school.

In many schools, both primary and secondary, there has been an attempt to create a spirit of collaboration among teachers, rather than a powerful hierarchy with a large distance between the head of the school and the more junior staff. Not all schools have succeeded and children and parents can both suffer if teachers in a school are feeling demoralised rather than buoyant about their work. Like many other professional workers, teachers need to know they are valued by the community they serve, rather than feel that they are not well thought of. The extensive industrial action of the mid-1980s began to open a rift between parents and teachers as the former, understandably, complained when their children were not being taught on a regular basis. Successive Education Acts, as well as developments like the GCSE and the introduction of more technical and vocational education, have put severe pressures on schools, and the senior people – heads and their deputies in particular – have had to expend a great deal of time keeping up their colleagues' morale.

Teachers and teaching

The teaching profession underwent a series of dramatic reforms in the 1960s, 1970s and 1980s. From the preparation of new recruits to the in-service training of experienced teachers, there were considerable changes in many aspects of professional work. Up to 1960 most non-graduate teachers received only two years of training and graduates were able to teach without any training at all. Initial training was stretched first to three years and then, from the late 1970s onwards, almost all recruits to both primary and secondary schools had taken a four-year course, either studying for a degree first and then taking a one-year postgraduate teacher-training course, or spending the whole four years on a degree course where the study of major teaching subjects and professional training were interwoven.

All governments since the 1950s have endeavoured to reduce class sizes. The result of this was a massive increase in the number of teachers recruited over the twenty-year period from the early 1950s to the early 1970s, during which time the teaching force doubled in size from 200,000 to 400,000. This increase in recruitment also coincided with a period when the numbers of pupils in schools were increasing because of the record level of births in the mid-1960s 'bulge'.

When the birth-rate began to fall, first slowly then, in the 1970s, rapidly, with a drop of one-third from the peak of 1964, the number of new teachers recruited also began to drop. The result of this roller-coaster graph of births has produced two effects. One was the closure and merger of many small schools as pupil rolls fell. The other was an odd distribution of age in the teaching profession. After a decade or more of seeing thousands of fresh-faced new young teachers entering the classroom, the average age of the profession began to go up until, by 1990, three out of every five teachers will be over 40. It will only be in the mid- to late 1990s, when rising pupil numbers once again require an influx of new teachers, that this predominantly middle-aged profession will change.

The major advantage to parents and children of a mature profession is that a considerable amount of accumulated experience is available compared with the inexperience of many of the young teachers newly recruited in the 1960s, who found themselves in the middle of major programmes of reorganisation in secondary schools. When the GCSE was introduced, in 1986, it was fortunate that there were so many seasoned professionals able to make sure it was launched as effectively as possible, given the many problems which accompanied its arrival.

Paradoxically, the disadvantage of a largely middle-aged profession can also be seen when changes occur. Teaching is a very busy job with many thousands of personal contacts in a single week. Teachers can soon develop patterns of teaching which, when significant changes occur, are very hard to modify. If a modern-language course based on grammar and translation is replaced by one emphasising speaking and writing the contemporary language, then some experienced teachers make the transition smoothly, while others use new curriculum materials but old-style and often inappropriate teaching methods.

The many rapid changes in society generally – especially the disappearance of unskilled jobs and the increasing emphasis on qualifications and the acquisition of skill and knowledge – have led many parents to raise their expectations of teachers and schools. In an area of high unemployment, much may depend on a young person obtaining a decent set of school-leaving credentials. This pressure for accountability led to the introduction in the 1986 Education Act of compulsory teacher appraisal. In our view, parents should not, as lay people, sit in on lessons to give teachers a mark out of ten like a Eurovision Song Contest jury, but if they are generally pleased with teachers, or if they have complained about poor teaching, then this should certainly figure in any professional appraisal of a teacher's work, provided it can be substantiated and is not based on malice, inadequate information or the views of an atypical minority.

One of the difficulties facing teachers, and indeed those who appraise them, is the many roles society expects them to play. First of all, they are supposed to be experts in one or more areas of subject matter, a narrower field for secondary compared with primary teachers. This in itself is extremely demanding, given the vast reservoir of knowledge already accumulated, with more being added on a daily basis. In addition to this principal role as transmitter of knowledge, skills and culture, teachers are also, especially if they teach in areas with severe social problems or a high crime rate, called upon to act as social worker. It is often a teacher who is the first person to see a battered or neglected child, for example, and many children rejected by their parents will confide in a teacher as the only adult in their circle offering stability and objective advice. Indeed, it is not unknown for teachers, especially in small tightly knit communities, to find themselves giving advice to parents facing problems as well.

In a busy week, teachers may find they are acting as appraiser (administering tests, marking books, writing references to employers), gaoler (making sure disaffected pupils do not play truant), nurse (giving first aid to an injured child), accountant (managing a budget), public-relations officer (talking to the local Press, meeting parents or governors) and student (attending in-service courses). It is no easy task to achieve success in each of, let alone all, these roles, especially in schools where the odds on failure are high. As a consequence, some of the problems which occur between teachers and parents can come about because a teacher is proficient in one field but not another. Excellent subject knowledge does not ensure understanding of a nervous child or a truculent adolescent, although some teachers can manifest both.

Sources of friction between parents and schools

In most schools, relationships between parents and teachers are at best positive and harmonious, at worst tolerable. Even in the best run schools, however, there may be occasional friction and tension, and in the worst schools these can become the norm. It is not possible to categorise every single case of a problem under a small set of headings, but here are some common examples.

Lack of information

On numerous occasions when an irate parent has telephoned or visited the school there has been a breakdown of communications at some stage. This can occur when pupils, especially young ones or adolescents who have gone into a monosyllabic phase, are given the main responsibility for messages from school to home or vice versa.

Some difficulties come about when letters are sent home via pupils. A few years ago we conducted an enquiry into home–school relationships and found that in some homes the letter given to the pupil had never been delivered. Sometimes it was still in a pocket, school bag or drawer when we called at the house. Once or twice the envelope stood on the mantelpiece unopened. Yet the letter might be about some important parents' evening, school trip or about the child's progress in class or lack of it. Well-organised schools try to ensure there is always a reply slip for important communications so they know if the letter has been delivered. One head, alarmed by the number of letters to parents which were not getting through, wrote to all his parents telling them of his concern – and sent the letter home via the pupils.

Other problems occur when parents simply do not understand some matter which teachers take for granted. If there have been changes in the law, such as the many brought about by the 1988 Education Reform Act, despite extensive newspaper, radio and television coverage, some parents will be oblivious to the consequences for schools. It is up to teachers and governors to keep them informed. The 1988 Act, for example, confirmed limited charging for features like instrumental music tuition and field courses, as well as the more publicised National Curriculum and tests of achievement at 7, 11, 14 and 16. Any changes occurring in schools as a result may be seen as the personal whim of the head or teacher unless schools explain what is happening.

There are often problems communicating with certain families. Perhaps the language used at home is not English and that is why some schools with a significant community of non-English speakers will see that key letters are translated into one or two of the most commonly occurring mother tongues. Sometimes there are several families which do not contain anyone who has been fortunate enough to study beyond the minimum school-leaving age, so even if there are no language problems, the demands of public examinations, such as the GCSE or A level, or the range of careers open to people with higher qualifications, are not fully understood.

Occasionally the lack of information is about very simple basic rules, conventions or needs – for example, about sports kit, uniform, educational trips, the punishment system or arrangements over the absence of pupils. Many schools now produce a simple handbook for parents which clarifies these matters.

Clash of values

Some difficulties occur when there is a mismatch between the values or aspirations of parents and those predominant in the school. This can be about a matter, like uniform, where a school may require it and some parents may be opposed to it, or vice versa. It can also happen over the curriculum if, for instance, parents feel too much or too little time is being devoted to a particular field.

Experience in a city primary school illustrates this problem well. Parents had heard from their children that they 'played'

in science lessons. At first sight this seems like a straightforward matter: learning is a serious business, parents become
dismayed if their children merely 'play around' when they
should be learning, and they should therefore tell the teachers
to get down to some serious work and all will be well. In fact,
when an evening event was arranged during which parents
had an opportunity to do the very experiments which their
children had done during the day, they soon realised that a
great deal of science could be learned from and through play
with a bouncing ball, magnetic figures in a game and soap-
bubble blowing. That learning could be enjoyable was something that many had not associated with their own childhood.

If parents can sometimes modify their views when they hear
a teacher's point of view, then the reverse is also certainly
true. A few years ago some teachers had not fully appreciated
that in certain cultures dancing, eating meat or girls baring
their legs in physical education lessons were regarded as
wrong. Meetings with parents, who were able to explain the
religious or cultural significance of something taken for
granted in Western societies, made such clashes less commonplace, though there is still further progress to be made in this
respect.

Another source of conflict can emerge when a school adopts
a new syllabus, different teaching methods or new set books.
Some parents believe that controversial matters should not be
discussed in school and may complain about subjects like
health education if drug or solvent abuse is mentioned, or if
political or religious issues are debated, or if a set text is read
in English literature which raises sensitive issues, such as
relationships between the sexes or bad language. Our own
view is that children cannot be shielded from the many controversial issues which are discussed in newspapers and on radio
and television. What is important is that teachers raise such
matters fairly and sensitively, as most indeed do, and at an
age and in a manner appropriate to the topic. Pretending that
differences of opinion and values do not exist in the world does
no service to young people who will soon have to make their
own informed judgements about many contemporary issues.
Teachers do need to recognise any parental sensitivities, but

45

equally parents need to understand that most teachers are doing their best to prepare children for adult life in a complex and problematical world.

Fair opportunities

If there is one matter which enrages pupil and parent alike, it is unfairness. Whenever children are interviewed about life in school, or when adults reminisce about their own childhood, cases of unfairness arouse great hostility.

Many instances of unfairness result from incidents in the classroom. Teachers may accuse a pupil of misbehaviour, dishonesty or untruthfulness, and great offence will be taken if the accusation is unjustified. Parents will then be told by an angry or tearful child of the nature of the injustice and will often be tempted to confront the teacher concerned. It is always wise to check first that one's child is giving an accurate account of events, otherwise a parent's indignation can soon turn to embarrassment when other witnesses confirm the teacher's story. None the less, parents should not hesitate to raise matters of genuine unfairness, especially in more serious cases, when, for example, someone has wrongly been accused of theft.

Alongside individual incidents, there can be a general sense of unfairness felt by whole groups of parents. Indeed, there is unfairness built into the educational system through the uneven distribution of resources mentioned above. What you get from school may be determined not so much by what you need as where you live or what group you belong to. There is frequently some usually unconscious bias in schools towards children from better-off homes, towards boys and against children from certain minority religious or ethnic groups. Studies of educational opportunities have shown that able children from poor social backgrounds are much less likely to go on to higher education than those of similar ability who come from professional families. Although this may be explained largely by factors mainly out of the control of schools, there may be too low expectations of children from less well-endowed homes.

Other reports suggest that girls often receive less attention than boys during lessons, although boys are usually reprimanded more than girls. Boys are three times more likely than girls to study subjects like physics to a high level; yet in schools where teachers make a special effort to encourage girls to widen their career choice, the position may not be so unfavourable. In one school, the head of physics went out of his way at the third-year stage, where pupils made critical options choices, to explain to girls that there were good opportunities for them in science, that many girls in the school had done well at physics and that, even if they did not wish to go on to university, there were interesting jobs as technicians which were often considered only as boys' jobs. The result was more or less equal numbers of GCSE and A-level boy and girl candidates. Girls obtain over 50 per cent of GCSE 'passes' (grades A to C), under 50 per cent of A-level passes, but only just over 40 per cent of degrees. Many able girls drop out; yet schools eager to see every pupil, boy or girl, given a fair chance to study to a high level, can achieve a great deal.

Many parents of children from ethnic minorities are also concerned that their own children should also have every chance to progress to further and higher education. Evidence from recent reports suggests that more black pupils than expected were put into remedial classes and one suggested explanation is again that teachers' expectations might have been too low. Parents who feel concerned that their child is not being encouraged to develop his or her talents fully should not hesitate to go to the school and discuss in a positive manner how a proper level of achievement can be secured.

Choice and selection

There are numerous occasions in education when someone has to make a choice. It may be that the onus is on the pupil to select from a set of options or to decide which of several activities to pursue. More likely to cause strife between parents and teachers are those occasions when it is the school which selects: who plays the lead in the school play, who is in the first team, who goes into a higher set or stream.

There are several critical points in children's schooling when choices must be made. The initial one comes when parents choose a school, and we explained in an earlier chapter how the appeals system works if their first choice is not met. Once a child is in a school, there are many routine choices to be made every single day, because most primary schools invite children to pick an activity or topic to which they personally wish to devote more time. Learning to choose from alternatives is in itself an important part of growing up, as indeed is learning to live with the consequences of your choice – like, for example, wishing you had opted for something else, or the occasional disappointment when your hopes cannot be fulfilled.

Depending on the policy for forming teaching groups within a school, there are also sensitive occasions, usually towards the end of each school year, when decisions are made about which teaching group a child will be in, either for all subjects or for each separate area of the curriculum, and which teachers he or she will have. Most secondary schools have, in recent years, moved away from a rigid streaming system where children were put into an A or a D stream for everything, irrespective of how talented they were in their various subjects. Nowadays, it is more likely that the early years of secondary schooling may operate via mixed-ability classes or that some form of 'banding' or 'setting' may take place.

'Banding' is a policy often favoured in larger schools. Faced with a ten-form or more entry and the evidence from several studies that the transfer rate between streams could be as low as 2 or 3 per cent, schools decided to set up, say, three broad bands of ability. Some 120 children of higher ability might be spread evenly across four classes in the top band; another 120 of average ability would be similarly accommodated in the middle band; allowing for two smaller remedial classes in the third band for children who had learning difficultes. 'Setting', by contrast, is the system whereby children are assigned to ability groups in each separate subject area, so that a pupil might be in set one for maths, set three for French, set two for science and so on. Each grouping policy has points in its favour, as well as disadvantages, but there will always be children at the borderline whose parents feel they are wrongly assigned. It is certainly a matter which parents may wish to discuss with a teacher when assignments to classes are made.

Pupil choices can be equally problematic. The National Curriculum established by the 1988 Education Reform Act does not determine the whole curriculum, so there will be points in a child's career when important choices must be made: whether to take up a second foreign language, to do separate or integrated sciences, to take A- or AS-level courses or opt for vocational subjects, such as catering, business studies or some combination of the two if that is permitted, as it often is in places like tertiary colleges.

Examinations pose similar problems of selection and choice. In the GCSE examination, for example, some subjects offer test papers at different levels. In modern languages, there are four papers which test speaking, listening, reading and writing, but these are offered at both a basic and a higher level, making eight papers in all. Pupils wishing to obtain higher grades must take something like six, seven or eight papers, while those settling for a more modest result could choose to take the four basic papers only.

Sometimes parents become very angry if the school suggests their child should concentrate on the basic papers, assuming that this is a put-down for the child. Usually a school would make such a recommendation only with the best interests of the child in mind. Some pupils might suffer if they had to do too much course work, for example, because some subjects require a great deal of continuous assessment throughout the two years leading up to GCSE. In other cases, a child might be demoralised by obtaining low marks on trial papers for the higher level and lose interest in the whole subject, instead of concentrating on the basic papers. Parents need to be satisfied, therefore, if they wish to insist their child takes everything at a higher level, that he or she will actually cope. Schools may, however, underestimate a pupil's ability, and it is perfectly proper for parents to ask to see the teacher responsible for GCSE entries to discuss such a matter part-way through their child's GCSE year.

Another problem can arise if a child's choice of course cannot be met. For instance, a pupil may wish to study a language like Russian, Spanish or Italian, take an A level in a field like philosophy or psychology, or learn a musical instrument such as the flute or trombone. Although there may be no chance at all of these aspirations being met, it is certainly a matter which parents can pursue, if necessary asking a parent-governor to raise it at a governors' meeting. There are now several possibilities, especially for older pupils. Home study and correspondence courses may be purchased which allow individuals to pursue subjects on their own or in small groups. Distance learning kits, often involving video cassettes as well as books or tapes, are also available in increasing numbers, and bodies like the Open College and the National Extension College, as well as commercial publishers, will produce these in a wider range of fields. Under the local school management scheme introduced by the 1988 Education Reform Act, governing bodies responsible for the school's own finances would have the option of paying for a limited amount of such self-help materials, though the same Act also permitted parents to be charged for such matters as instrumental tuition.

Personal relationships

Within any community, the quality of the relationships between its members is crucial to the general well-being of everyone. Among the greatest sources of distress to both children and their parents are those occasions when a pupil and a teacher simply do not get on together, or, more rarely, if a breakdown in relationships among the staff, especially if there is strife between the head and the teachers, begins to affect the children. In such cases, parents need to ask themselves a number of questions before taking action. The first is whether or not their child is the only one to feel unhappy about the relationship. There is a difference between the teacher who is well liked and respected by everyone except one's own child and the teacher who has poor relationships with most or all pupils. In the latter case, other parents might wish to join someone seeking to take the matter further.

Sometimes the problem can be relationships between pupils. In most such cases, adults tend to leave youngsters to sort matters out for themselves, and few parents seek to intervene as their children acquire new friends and grow cooler towards earlier ones, on the grounds that choosing those you wish to associate with is an important part of learning to live in society. The difficulty comes when certain types of relationship occur.

One of the most difficult to handle can be when parents have an uneasy feeling that their child is associating with the 'wrong crowd'. There are few out-and-out undesirables in most schools, but parents can get distressed if their child is friendly with pupils who show no interest in academic work or who have a reputation for disrupting lessons, or, worse, if he or she goes round with people known to be engaged in something seamy, like drugs, under-age drinking or theft. By and large, this is a matter they will usually need to discuss at home, but it may be worth raising at school and it should certainly be discussed with the head or teaching staff if undesirable activities are thought to be occurring on or near the school premises.

Of greater concern is an issue like bullying. Some children become miserable because they have been made a scapegoat at school, the butt of abuse or intimidation from other pupils, sometimes just one. Many parents are reluctant to be thought wimpish or over-protective and fear that their child's position may become even worse if he or she is labelled a sneak. They may also assume, wrongly, that senior teachers might not be prepared to keep such matters confidential. Heads and deputies in primary schools, their counterparts in secondary schools, as well as teachers who are head of a year-group or form tutors with responsibility for pastoral care, are used to being asked by parents to keep a complaint or enquiry confidential. It is part of their job to investigate sensitive matters in a discreet way without putting any particular child in the spotlight.

Assessment

During the last few years, the whole question of assessment has assumed a very high profile, especially since the GCSE was reformed and tests for 7, 11, 14 and 16-year-olds were introduced in the 1988 Education Reform Act. This matter is dealt with fully in another book in this series (*Testing and Assessment* by Charles Desforges, 1989), so we shall only comment briefly on it here.

Assessment can consist of anything from a raised eyebrow, a smile or a single word like 'good' or 'rubbish', up to a full set of three-hour test papers taken under examination conditions. Most assessment of children's progress takes place on a regular basis throughout the school year, rather than on a single ritualised occasion at the end of it. Thus a routine aspect, such as the marking of homework or classwork, occupies more time than the appraisal of a GCSE paper, though the latter is much more important in the public mind.

Friction between parents and teachers can occur if a child's work is not being marked, if a grade is given which the child considers unfair, or, in the case of *profiling*, where grades of A to E may be given on a series of behaviour and personality traits, such as 'co-operativeness' or 'persistence' – as well as on academic achievements – if a child is stereotyped as 'grade C' for everything.

If children's work is not being marked at all or is considered to be unfairly graded, then this is certainly a matter which parents are entitled to raise with the teachers concerned. Teacher assessments are an integral part of examinations like the GCSE, the Certificate of Pre-Vocational Education taken by pupils at 17, and national tests. It is difficult for parents to know, if they are not familiar with the field, whether a mark of 12 out of 20 for a literary essay or a grade C for a chemistry practical test or a German oral, is an appropriate one, and parents need to raise these issues in a sensible way. In some parts of the United States, when too big a fuss was made by some parents about subjective marking of essays or assignments, many teachers simply used more multiple choice and yes/no or true/false type questions, because this would reduce or eliminate arguments. Teachers are usually trying to grade pupils' work fairly, but all human judgement is open to question, so parents who are really concerned about an assessment issue should make an appointment to see the teacher concerned.

Trouble-shooting

This chapter has tried to convey some of the complexities of school organisation and examine a few of the more common sources of friction between parents and teachers. In any society, misunderstandings and tensions are bound to occur, so parents need not feel guilty if they find themselves immersed in one. Frequently, we have mentioned making contact with someone in the school and the key person or lever puller may not be the same in all schools. We shall return in Chapter 5 to the question of resolving difficulties when we consider specific cases where parents might wish to contact the school. For the present, the following check-list might be helpful:

- If a visit to school is needed, telephone or write first to make an appointment.
- Check with the school secretary whether you should discuss this with the head or deputy, the class teacher or form tutor, or a subject specialist.
- Bear in mind that most people you want to see may have a full teaching programme, so you may have to fit a visit into their non-teaching time, unless they can free themselves of a commitment. Equally they should try to accommodate any difficulty you might have with job or family commitments.
- Be clear in your mind what the main purpose of your visit is. There may be more than one, but it is sometimes helpful to write a letter spelling out that you want to discuss, say, your child's maths and science or his or her unhappiness over some matter. Make it clear also if you want this to be in strict confidence. It usually will be, but teachers need to know if your child is aware you are coming to school, or if they may discuss the matters you raise with certain other teachers.
- If you are making a complaint, check all the facts first with your own child and other parents if they are involved.
- Before you leave the school, ensure you know what action is being taken, if any is needed.
- Try to anticipate problems so that crisis visits are unnecessary. If you do feel stressed about going to the school, try to be more at ease about it so that the discussion is as positive as possible from your point of view and not unnecessarily acrimonious.

Chapter 4
INVOLVING PARENTS

We have tended to emphasise problems of parents understanding or being able to come to terms with the organisation of schools in the last chapter, but parents usually find that most of their contacts with schools are positive. In this chapter we shall review some of the many worthwhile links between home and school which have been developed from the moment when parents choose a school to the day that pupils leave it.

Choosing a school

Most of us have to make choices of an institution at some time in our lives and selecting a school is one of the most common. We often have little say in which hospital treats our ailments, which county council handles our local affairs or which police force investigates our crimes, but we usually have more influence on which church we wish to attend, which doctor or dentist should treat us, or which school will educate our children, especially if we live in a city. In rural areas we may have a very narrow range of such options, frequently just one.

It would be easy if there were some foolproof school-appraisal list, some super sniffer which could detect the best school for any particular child. To the outsider, schools can often appear very similar to each other, and what appeals to an adult may not satisfy a child. One former chief education officer advised parents simply to follow their instinct, arguing that, if a bunch of dead daffodils greeted you in the entrance hall, this might indicate a lack of care about other more important matters. The difficulty of this approach is that a gleaming surface does not always guarantee that all is well beneath it, and sometimes a head may be good at public relations but less competent at running an effective school.

There are different factors at work when parents choose a primary or secondary school or a tertiary college, dealing with all education in a region for students over 16. Factors affecting choice of an infant or first school often concern such matters as how far a 5-year-old would have to travel, whether a busy road has to be crossed, whether older brothers or sisters went to the same school and, most importantly, whether the atmosphere is warm and friendly or cold and intimidating.

As children grow older, some of these factors still apply, but others begin to figure more prominently and pupils themselves are more likely to be involved in the decision. Children transferring at the age of 11 to a secondary school are on the verge of adolescence: that period in their lives when the peer group, one's mates, becomes important to them. Thus, at this stage they may well want to go to the same school as certain of their primary school friends. Parents may be less concerned about bus journeys and crossing roads and more interested in assessment results at GCSE or help with careers and success in further and higher education.

When transfer occurs at 16, pupils usually want to have a very significant stake in the choice themselves. They are much more likely to ask their own questions about whether vocational courses are offered in fields such as business studies or catering, what A levels are available and whether their own favoured subject combination is possible. They will also want to know more about tutorial guidance, social and recreational facilities and the success rates of former students. Parents may even take a back seat at this stage. There is quite a transfer out of private schools, or conventional schools with sixth forms, at the 16-plus stage if pupils have the opportunity to attend a tertiary college instead.

As we explained in Chapter 1, schools are now obliged to give parents much more information than would previously have been necessary. However, it is important for parents to become involved with a likely school for their child in a more positive way than merely perusing a prospectus. A school which a child might attend should certainly be visited, and very often schools nowadays hold open evenings for prospective parents. If these consist solely of a stand-up talk by the head, it is not unreasonable for parents to ask for a chance to see the classrooms, facilities such as gymnasium, drama studio or laboratories. Although not everyone can be an expert on what a well-stocked chemistry lab needs, it is not too difficult to sense whether the environment seems attractive, to detect a school where children's work is proudly displayed or to pick up whether the head and teachers seem enthusiastic or are 'pre-retired' – that state in which someone has died in the job and been allowed to stay on posthumously.

Really brave schools will even have pupils present so that parents and potential recruits can hear directly from them what they do and whether they like the school. It is useful to obtain the pupil's view of a school and worth tracking down families who already have children in a school under consideration. Although some may exaggerate problems or their disaffection with a school – which might mean lack of interest in any schooling not just their own particular school – most will be honest about their experiences. There is often a well-established and clear folklore about a school, even if there are individual dissenters. Informants who are in that adolescent phase when obtaining more than a monosyllabic grunt is a major triumph, often say little more than 'It's all right', but this may be the nearest they ever come, at that stage in their lives, to ecstasy.

At the stage of transfer from the primary to the secondary phase of schooling, some schools will arrange quite elaborate means of involving parents and future pupils. Often both primary feeder schools and the receiving secondary schools will have appointed liaison teachers, whose job is to make sure the transition is as smooth as possible. Between them, they may arrange not just a school visit for pupils but a complete programme. Primary pupils have not usually had the opportunity to work in a science laboratory, use a fully equipped gymnasium or learn a language like German or Spanish. One secondary school gives children from local primary schools a full day of such lessons as a taste of secondary schooling. A few days later, their parents are invited to an evening meeting. It seems to give a great deal of valuable information to both parents and pupils, as well as reduce anxiety about going to the larger senior school.

Parent—teacher activities

It would be easy to assume that there was nowadays no need to involve parents very much in the life of the school, because parent-governors can raise on their behalf any important issues which might arise. This would be a grave error. The fact that, by law, from two to five parents must be members of the school's governing body means that hundreds of others will not have this privilege and will need to feel party to what the school is doing.

During the 1960s and 1970s, much greater awareness of the importance of links between home and school led to many schools establishing parent—teacher associations, or PTAs as they are usually called. Some schools named them 'parents' associations' on the grounds that they were really for parents and should not be dominated by teachers. Other schools have excellent relationships with parents without necessarily setting up a formal PTA structure. It is possible in one school to have a high level of involvement of parents without having a PTA, and in another a low level despite having a PTA, because the assumption in the latter is that the annual dinner dance is all that is necessary for good communication and positive relationships.

Parent—teacher associations have been established for several different reasons and can be quite distinct from each other in terms of what they actually do. Among common activities are the following.

Social events

These are usually evening or weekend affairs with the emphasis on parents and teachers mixing in a friendly relaxed manner. They may take the form of a dance, buffet, fête or excursion. There is no pretence about discussing school affairs, although these may be talked about incidentally. In one new housing estate, the PTA built the school a swimming-pool and had its own PTA clubhouse. As there was little social provision on the estate itself, the PTA activities became the local leisure programme and many people attended as guests even if they did not have any children in the school at that time.

Fundraising

One of the best-known functions of PTAs is their ability to raise money. Since education is supposed to be free according to the 1944 Education Act – with the exception of the charges for such items as longer field-trips and instrumental music tuition, mentioned above, which were legitimised by the 1988 Education Reform Act – it does mean that such fundraising must be voluntary. Any appearance of compulsion would be illegal unless the school is a private one where fees are charged which can be varied or increased. Traditionally, PTAs have raised cash for what could be considered 'extras', although the nature of these has never been specified. In one context, a microcomputer might be seen as a luxury extra, in another as virtually essential.

There has been concern, since the education cuts of the late 1970s and early 1980s, that such PTA bounties have increasingly been used for the basics of education, such as books, paper or paint, rather than for video recorders, cassette players or whatever else may be regarded more as a bonus than the basic fabric of teaching. Some PTAs have protested that the local authority should provide essential materials as a matter of course. For those secondary schools and large primary schools which are now responsible for their own finances since the 1988 Act, the same convention should apply, and parents are entitled to protest if they feel their school is under-funded according to their local authority's funding formula, and can only run on what are virtually parental subscriptions. The LEA funding formula is known to the governors and is not confidential.

Once money has been raised, a PTA can either give it to the school as a free gift, in which case it is up to the head and the governors to determine how it is spent, or they can attach strings by designating what it should be spent on.

Curriculum evenings

Many schools use their PTA in a more deliberately educational manner by asking it to sponsor evening meetings for parents. It is, of course, not necessary to have a PTA to do this and most schools will arrange a series of meetings for parents when they can come in to see teachers, discuss their child's progress or hear about some new development, like the latest information on the National Curriculum or a new test or examination.

When schools occasionally claim that they have organised such evenings or meetings and few parents bothered to turn up, there is often a simple explanation. In one school, teachers believed that many parents lacked interest in their children's schooling because they did not come to evening meetings. When we interviewed a sample of parents, we found that some mothers worked what was known as the 'twilight shift' in the local factory – that is, they had a part-time evening job from 5 until 9 o'clock. Others had small children and no babysitter or looked after an elderly or infirm relative. Some were one-parent families, so they could not share these duties with a partner.

Sometimes an evening meeting is not popular because of the form it takes. Experience has shown that parents are more likely to turn out on a wet November evening if (a) their own children are involved, and (b) they themselves are active rather than passive spectators. Two primary schools in a similar part of town had parents' evenings at about the same time of the year: one event was packed, the other almost deserted. The near-empty evening was one at which the head, well-known for waffling audiences into deep sleep, was scheduled to give yet another tedious address on primary mathematics. The full house was for the latest of an occasional series in the other school on primary curriculum, when parents would be given the opportunity to do the actual science experiments that their children had been carrying out that day.

There are many activities which are more likely to engage parents' interest than the set-piece lecture. These include parents doing what their children do – difficult if it is an A-level physics class but not impossible if it concerns primary science (as above), where the room can be laid out with experiments and a discussion can follow; or a modern language lesson where parents go through lesson one so that they see the filmstrip or repeat the phrases just as their children might.

Another possibility is to see an actual lesson. This can take many forms, such as watching and then discussing a specially made videotape of, say, a drama or science lesson. Alternatively, it might be done as a role-play with the school hall laid out half as a classroom, half with seats for parents. The teacher takes a typical lesson in the 'classroom' part of the hall and the parents can wander in to see what their children are actually doing. One school simply holds an open day when parents can go into any classroom, lab or gymnasium and watch any lesson. With the many new developments in education in recent years and more fresh initiatives every year, this is the kind of activity that should be offered in every school, not just those that have the initiative to implement it now.

The more straightforward parents' evening, where parents meet teachers to discuss their child's progress, is often unsatisfactory from a parent's point of view. Many complain about long waiting times, lack of confidentiality or the brevity of their consultation. Some of these complaints can be met by an appointments system and by inviting parents who feel they need longer time or want to talk in private to come at a different time or under different conditions. There is nothing worse for a nervous parent wishing to talk over a serious problem than to discover a teacher looking anxiously at his watch because things are running late and that the next three couples are waiting in line, able to hear every word of the conversation.

There are numerous other ways to allow parents and teachers to meet. One primary school in a very difficult city area, where there was a high crime rate and many families experienced severe social problems, ran a book club from 3 until 4 o'clock once a month. Children were able to bring money each week and save up until the local bookshop owner came in on the first Tuesday of each month, when they could spend their money. A wide selection of books was on hand, some with slight marks on them, so they were available at reduced prices. Parents collecting their children were invited along as well to discuss likely books with teachers and the bookseller. The result was that homes which usually had no books at all acquired valuable reading material, parents heard their children read and teachers saw the reading scores of their pupils climb slowly in a district where every educational advantage would help children who were going to run up against all kinds of difficulties in their later lives. The school also acquired an excellent library, because the grateful bookseller gave books to the value of 10 per cent of what the children spent each month.

Parents in the classroom

Primary schools, in particular, have often involved parent helpers in the classroom. When there are lots of shoe-laces to tie, sad and happy stories of pets, family members and birthday presents to hear, having an extra adult or two can be a great help to the teacher. Infant schools often have two or three parents in a classroom, some giving casual help or talking to children about their work. It is a matter which must be handled skilfully, because most parents are not professionally trained.

One Cornish head, who pioneered the idea and usually had up to 50 parents willing to help in his school, used to say that the parents must always be clearly under the supervision of the teacher and must only be asked to do what a concerned, thoughtful mother or father would do at home. In his school, a grandparent who was a retired bank manager collected all the dinner money, a father who was a qualified swimming teacher assisted in the swimming lessons and several parents who were experts at cookery, embroidery, crocheting, knitting or country dancing helped out in lessons, bringing a valuable extra dimension as well as increased commitment to the school. The head used the analogy of a visit to a farm. If teachers take a class to see a farm, they prepare for the visit, brief the children, arrange the transport and capitalise on the children's experiences in future lessons, but when they are actually on the farm it is the farmer who shows them round and explains how the farm works. Using parents who had interest and expertise was, he argued, very similar.

Other schools, both primary and secondary, have used parents as extra pairs of eyes and hands on excursions (although not giving them sole charge of the class). Some have invited parents to help with the library or resources collection

– for example, mounting and filing collections of newspaper cuttings under various headings. Some schools invite parents who are in jobs to come along to their employment fairs, when pupils move round stalls finding out about different careers. Many secondary schools can rustle up parents who are nurses, police officers, secretaries, building workers, garage employees or who work in the major professions or run a small business.

Helping children learn

A few years ago we conducted an enquiry into parents' attitudes to their children's education which included several hundred interviews. One of the questions we asked was: what, if anything, parents had done to prepare their children for starting school? Most told us that they had done nothing about the academic side of school because they had been given the message that trying to help at home would probably jeopardise their children's life chances. So we asked teachers why they tried to put off parents of children under 5 from preparing them for school. We were given only one answer: parents teach capital letters and schools begin with small letters. Since that time there has been a much better awareness of the positive effect parents can have and many schools, far from discouraging parents and making them feel somehow unclean and guilty about assisting in their children's learning, go out of their way to encourage them to help.

Although successive Education Acts in the 1980s gave parents more rights, they did not give them more information about how to help with their children's learning; that was assumed to be an inevitable consequence rather than the principal purpose of legislation aimed at improving matters for parents. Increasingly, schools themselves and sometimes local authorities take responsibility for informing parents.

The process can begin before formal schooling has commenced. Many primary school heads nowadays write a more welcoming letter, suggesting activities which would benefit a child, to prospective parents than might have been the case formerly. The letter might point out that if children are interested in letter shapes, the school will teach small letters first, that parents often like to read stories to children and point to the pictures. This will show a child what are sometimes called 'pre-reading' skills, quite simple matters such as the need to turn pages, the fact that pictures are related to the text or that reading can be fun as well as informative. The letter may also suggest that helping with shopping or counting money, fingers and toes, birthday cards or peas in a pod, all help children develop a sense of number. It may also mention that it is helpful if children can recognise common colours, tie their own shoe-laces or have a rough idea of what time of day it is. Emphasising the positive seems much better for home–school relations than warning parents off.

Once children have started school, parents can help them at home by hearing them read, for example. There are many schemes specially developed for this purpose. Some of the major publishers have produced readers, as well as number or science books, which parents can buy in city bookshops and which are specially designed for an adult and child to work on together. Several local authorities, as well as schools or other agencies, have themselves taken responsibility for showing parents how they can help young children, especially with reading. In the London area, the PACT (Parents and Children and Teachers) scheme for reading and the LEA 'IMPACT' scheme for mathematics were developed as methods of briefing parents how to hear their children read, keep records, correct errors, explain problems, discuss progress. Paired reading schemes have also emerged, whereby parent and child read out loud together.

One or two councils have appointed home–school liaison tutors whose job it is not only to deal with social problems, but also to assist parents who want to help children at home. If neither school nor local authority offers such schemes in the early stages of schooling, parents who wish for it should not hesitate to press for systematic help of this kind to be provided. It is especially vital for children who have some degree of difficulty with learning, but all can benefit, and the excuse that parents will attempt to push children beyond their limit has rarely been substantiated in the many schemes already established. Indeed, most programmes are simply attempting to capitalise on the natural goodwill and common sense which already inform relationships in many families.

In some areas now, the local authority has set up a whole series of family workshops where parents, grandparents, relatives and children themselves can all attend. These are often aimed at mothers of young pre-school children in particular, but they can be wider. For example, younger children might be finger-painting and older ones making models, while their parents engage in crafts, such as pottery or weaving. The wide spread of community schools, open to all, has encouraged the whole family approach.

Once children are older, the pattern of helping is bound to change. Many parents will not have the grasp of subject matter necessary when primary children study science or when secondary pupils are preparing for their GCSE examinations. Buying suitable books is one way of helping and although encyclopaedias are popular, and indeed valuable in certain contexts, advice from teachers may identify a quite different set of useful background books. Taking one's child to the local library is also a valuable initiation which parents can perform.

A dilemma comes for parents at the GCSE stage, where, increasingly, marks for course-work undertaken during the years leading up to the public examination at 16 will help to determine the final grade. Course-work can earn between about 20 and 100 per cent of the marks, depending on the subject and syllabus. The fairness of allowing work done over a long period to count towards the final mark is counterbalanced by the unfair distribution of opportunities for different children. Some have access to large public or private libraries, and can seek help from parents who themselves were educated to a high level; while others have few local or domestic resources and their parents may have left education at the minimum school-leaving age.

The problem for parents is knowing what is legitimate help and what might be regarded as cheating. Since there are no written prescriptions, common sense again must be the guide. Writing something for one's child, determining the nature of the work or solving all the maths problems for him or her is cheating. Discussing the work, answering occasional questions or suggesting where information may be found is not. No doubt some unscrupulous parents will overstep the mark and write their children's work for them and in many cases be found out. Although it would serve them right if they consequently obtained a low grade for their offspring, it would eventually discredit the whole move towards recognising children's course-work and so parents of goodwill should not overstep the mark.

In general, the advice usually offered to parents during their children's school career includes the following:

Do
- support and encourage;
- treat learning as enjoyable and worthwhile;
- operate 'little and often', rather than for occasional long tedious sessions;
- ask where possible rather than tell, so that children learn to think for themselves;
- refer them to books and other sources of information not just yourself;
- ask the advice of teachers and keep them informed;
- invite other members of the family to show an interest.

Don't
- belittle children's efforts;
- push them beyond their limits;
- stress your own ambitions;
- concentrate on failures at the expense of praising successes;
- lose patience if your child does not grasp something immediately;
- cover material which the child will soon be doing at school and then find he or she is bored by it in class;
- force on children methods you used in your own schooling and then discover the school uses different ones – check first;
- regard learning as an Olympic event, like synchronised swimming, which you and your child must win.

Parent-governors

Hundreds of thousands of parents now belong to school governing bodies, which, as we pointed out in Chapter 1, are now much more powerful than they were a few years ago following the 1986 and 1988 Education Acts. Every school, depending on its size, will have between two and five governors who are parents. Since parent-governors constitute a quarter of the whole board, are full members and are able to give the point of view of children and fellow parents, they should be a powerful force. Yet parents who became governors often confess to a feeling of impotence and many say they would like to know how to be more effective.

The problem can begin with the very first meeting. Research into parent-governors conducted at Exeter University by Dr Michael Golby has shown that many parents have little idea of what to expect when they first became governors. Often they are surprised to discover that, inside the first 30 seconds of their opening meeting, the clerk calls for nominations and the chair and vice-chair for the year have been elected. Feeling new to the game, they do not like to protest and it is only later they discover that two local politicians have hijacked the two positions at their political caucus meeting the night before. Parents new to a meeting need to pluck up enough courage, therefore, to ask the clerk to the governors if there could be a short discussion of the whole question of chair and vice-chair before names are actually produced, so that members can give the matter proper thought.

As full members of the governing body, parents have the rights that go with the office. They may attend all meetings, only exceptionally – if their own child were under discussion, for example, or if they owned a business which might benefit financially from orders placed by the school – would they have to leave the room for an item. They will find themselves on interviewing sub-committees selecting new teachers or even the head, may have to visit County Hall with a governors' deputation, will be invited to certain special events, may be asked to join a working party on some matter, and will be expected to discuss the annual governors' report and attend the annual meeting when it is discussed by parents.

One of the difficulties many parents face on governing bodies is not having the confidence of someone professionally engaged in education. Parents often confess in private interview that they are apprehensive about joining in a debate in case they put their foot in it, or that they are afraid to stop the meeting and ask for an explanation of some item in case they look foolish. Parents are on governing bodies as the voice of those whose children are at the sharp end of the process, not as a world expert on the psychology of learning disabilities or the evaluation of a new curriculum. Thus, if parents find they are on an interviewing panel for a teaching post, they should simply try to envisage each candidate teaching children like their own, and their questions may reflect this vantage point. There will be people present who can advise the panel about each applicant's professional expertise or ask more technical questions. For fear of saying too much, many parent-governors say too little and are self-effacing to the point of becoming invisible.

Some parents are unused to the ways of a committee. Certainly most of us experience a real shock when we first join a committee, especially if it is over-formal. Committees exist to make sure business is properly transacted. In order to do this, a degree of formality is necessary, but it should not become overwhelming. Certain items are essential. Someone must chair the meeting; someone else must record the decisions. So that members know what to expect, they should receive the relevant paperwork and an agenda a few days in advance. Anything more fancy than that may be an unnecessary hindrance to the efficiency of the governing body, especially if people use excessively pompous language, and talk like a bureaucratic version of the speaking clock instead of a fellow human being.

Parents should not feel intimidated about getting an item on the agenda. It is often assumed by committees that the agenda is delivered by magic and that the mysteries of its assembly are beyond ordinary mortals like themselves. All one has to do to get an item on the agenda is ask the chair of the governing body to agree it. It is customary to provide a short paper when appropriate, but this is certainly not the sort of literary masterpiece that should require more than a few minutes of effort. For example, if fellow parents are concerned about the provision of a crossing warden outside the school gate before and after school and ask a parent-governor to do something about it, then a short note would suffice, saying, '*Road Safety*: A number of parents have asked whether a lollipop man/lady could be provided now that the road outside the school has become busier.' If the chair agrees, it could appear on the agenda just in that form for the governors to discuss, and the head or the LEA could advise about costs and other implications.

As we pointed out in Chapter 1, parent-governors are not duty bound to vote or act as a separate caucus. Governors must work as a body, not as individuals or pressure groups. Therefore, the parent-governor who, on being elected, told the head she wanted to inspect the school immediately was in the wrong. Governors' meetings will discuss which governors should have a turn at visiting the school on a more formal basis, and each member will have a chance to do this. If a governing body splits into four quite separate groups – as 'parents', 'teachers', 'local authority' and 'community' – it will never work as a harmonious whole.

Among the many positive contributions parents can make are the following:

- reporting the views of fellow parents (preferably from all social groups not only those of their own circle or part of the catchment area);
- asking their own and other children's opinions on matters which are not confidential;
- making sure that the reasons behind decisions are based on the needs of the community, not bureaucratic convenience (in one school, which had not been painted for years, governors were told there was no point in complaining because many other schools were in the same position: a parent-governor insisted on making a complaint and the school was in fact painted shortly afterwards);
- interviewing parents whose children are about to come into the school (one secondary school found that parents were

more likely to tell parent-governors than teachers about matters such as the high cost of uniforms and their children's anxiety about being bullied).

One other area where parent-governors can play a valuable part is at the annual meeting which governors are obliged to hold specially for parents. At this meeting, parents must discuss the governors' annual report and they may, if they wish, pass a motion on any matter which concerns them and which governors must then consider. One service parent-governors can perform is to help improve on attendance and interest. Some governors have produced reports of such monumental tedium that no one wanted to discuss them. Parent-governors can read the draft version as if they are typical parents and suggest ways of making it more 'user friendly', as computer jargon has it. If attendance is poor, they can also suggest ways of improving it. Perhaps parents would prefer the meeting to be combined with a social event, or with the sort of evening, described earlier, where they can see what children do in school or address questions about the school's health education programme, school uniform or other central matters. It is up to parent-governors to convey to other non-parent members what a typical mother or father would like on such an occasion. Parent-governors wishing to know more about the job might like to read the handbook we have written for school governors: E. C. Wragg and J. A. Partington, *A Handbook for School Governors* (Routledge, 1989).

Parent power

It has been fashionable to talk, in recent years, about 'parent power' in education. The assumption is that, once mobilised, parents can, as a group, trample all over politicians, heads, teachers or bureaucrats and determine the course of education. Parents in Britain still have fewer formal powers and rights than their counterparts in some other countries, but they can still, nevertheless, achieve a great deal.

One of the most effective means open to them is to write a personal letter to their MP or county or city councillor. Parents are electors, so when they write to their elected members expressing their concern, the latter must listen. Nothing concentrates the mind as much as the thought of one's meal ticket disappearing over the horizon. The mother who wrote a personal letter to her county councillor whose education committee was threating to take away a teacher from the local village school and began, 'I am so angry I have stopped my washing to write you this letter, so please do me the courtesy of reading it', was more likely to get a response than if she had signed a petition or merely grumbled at home.

In order to be effective, parents need to be sure of their facts, willing to write letters or attend meetings and able to organise themselves. Resisting a school closure is a good example of this. Those that have managed it have usually made sure their case is as strong as it can be, have written to key members of the county council or its education committee, and, most importantly, actually attended the meeting at which crucial decisions were going to be made. Most councils have a schools sub-committee which would be the first group to confirm a proposal to close or reorganise a school. Parents, like other members of the public, are entitled to attend such meetings under the terms of the 1960 Public Bodies (Admissions to Meetings) Act. If they are present in the public gallery at the moment when the critical debate takes place, it is more likely their case will be treated sympathetically than if they are absent. Really shrewd parents always invite important members of the relevant committee to visit their school. It is much harder to close a school you have visited than one which is merely a name on a list.

Similarly, if parents feel a school is being resistant to their strongly held wishes, it is better to act as a group than as individuals. However, in all these cases it is important that people are on safe ground and sure of their facts. On one occasion a group of angry parents working on hearsay raised a fuss at an open meeting in a secondary school about the English teaching. 'Why,' someone demanded, 'are pupils not being entered for GCSE English Literature papers?' Another parent stood up and added, 'And why don't they read any Shakespeare?' When the head of the English replied that 36 pupils were in fact taking the literature examination that year, and all were reading *The Merchant of Venice*, their case collapsed and they looked foolish. Better would have been to discard that particular point and concentrate on criticisms of the English teaching which could be substantiated.

There is a need, however, for parent power to be sensibly directed; with power comes responsibility. If parents are to exercise their collective power, it must be for the common good, not out of spite, whim or the desire to secure most of the school's resources for their own children or their particular prejudices. The naked exercise of power is ugly and benefits no one, least of all the children the school is meant to serve. Much better is a positive partnership between parents and teachers, such as was described earlier in this chapter. That is the fruitful use of parental energy.

Chapter 5
DIFFICULT PROBLEMS

Even in the best-managed schools, parents can find they have difficulties for which they were unprepared. What do you do if your child is being bullied? Suppose you think your child's teacher is incompetent, should you complain and will your child then suffer? If there is a problem, who is the person to deal with it – the head, the deputy or the class teacher? There are no omni-purpose answers to these questions, but we offer a few suggestions below about problems which have come to our attention during the last few years. The actual details given are based on true cases, although the identities of the teachers, parents and schools are not revealed. These case-studies cannot be exhaustive, but they do illustrate some of the actions that parents may need to take in difficult circumstances.

Problem One

Our PTA has raised money for the primary school but the head never spends it on things we feel are appropriate. She has a powerful personality and most of us are too apprehensive to tell her about our concerns. For example, she spent some of the money on the school field visit, paying for children to stay in hotels when we felt it would be less extravagant to go to a field-centre.

Comment: If a PTA raises money and gives it to the head without strings attached, then she is entitled to spend it on what she judges to be important, although anyone with any sense would keep the PTA in the picture. One possibility would be for parents to ask for a shopping list *in advance* of raising cash. Then they could decide, when giving money, which items – a cassette recorder, a microcomputer or some musical instruments, for example – it should be spent on.

However, this does not get to the root of the basic problem, which is the unnecessary awe that the PTA feels towards the head. You need to get up off your collective knees and solve this problem. Perhaps the chair and one other member of the committee should go and see her to discuss this very matter. There is no need to duck the issue. As ratepayers you are paying her salary, and even Genghis Khan was careful not to bite the hand that fed him. Following the 1988 Education Reform Act, schools which have local financial management must, in any case, have much closer liaison between the head and governors, including parent-members, on how money is spent. Incidentally, do not assume that the head has wasted money staying in hotels during field-trips. It can sometimes be quite cheap out of season for a party of schoolchildren. Again, under local financial management, this is a question which could be asked at a governors' meeting.

Problem Two

My 7-year-old son has just moved up to the junior school and is very unhappy because one older boy is regularly bullying him. He does not want me to make a fuss and, since he is new to the school, I do not want to appear to be an over-protective parent, but the other day his dinner money was stolen.

Comment: You now have two reasons to go into the school. Bullying is bad enough but extortion, the taking of money by force, is a crime which must be dealt with even if committed by young children. Telephone the head and explain what has happened, making an appointment to go into school if necessary. Heads are quite used to checking up on such stories and taking action in a discreet way without embarrassing your child or breaking a professional confidence – and you can reassure your child on this.

Before you go to see the head just check up on your son's own behaviour. Has he been pestering older children or been a nuisance, inviting an aggressive response? If he has, then ask him to be careful about his own behaviour in his new school, otherwise he may not make friends. However, he may well not have been immature himself, in which case he should not be made to feel guilty at having the misfortune to run into an older bully. No school with untreated bullying can be a happy community, so you will probably find the head is anxious to stamp it out quickly. Should there be no action, you could always ask for it to be discussed at a governors' meeting, because governors are responsible for conduct in a school, but it is unlikely this will be necessary. However, do not hesitate to be persistent about getting bullying stamped out.

Problem Three

My daughter, aged 10, is dyslexic; at least I think she is because she seems to get her letters back to front and makes a complete mess of some words. One or two members of my side of the family had similar problems with reading and writing. Her class teacher tries to be helpful, but I wondered if she ought to go to a special school of some sort, as her present teacher seems to be willing rather than expert on the subject.

Comment: This has been a common problem for many years and although provision is better now, it is by no means perfect, varying considerably across the country. There are two views about children with special educational needs. One is that they should go to a special school where the staff will be experts in their particular problem or handicap. The other is that they should, where possible, be educated alongside other children of their age, but be given special help. This was the view taken by the 1981 Education Act.

In the short term, you should ask the head if there is any specialist help available. Some local authorities provide what are called peripatetic teachers, whose job is to travel round several schools giving individual or small group tuition. Under local financial management, a school would be able to buy in such help from its own resources and the governors should have a policy on this.

In the longer term, you need to bear in mind that next year your daughter will move up to the secondary school. You should ask the local authority for an assessment of her learning needs. This will involve an educational psychologist testing and interviewing her before drawing up a statement, describing what would be best for her. Under the 1981 Education Act, you are entitled to see this statement. If you do not agree with the recommendation, you can appeal, if necessary, all the way to the Secretary of State.

The educational psychologist may well recommend a secondary school which has special provision for dyslexics or for children who need specialist help. This can involve what is called 'withdrawal' or 'extraction' for an hour or two a day, when your daughter would receive individual help from a specialist. This teacher would also liaise with the many teachers who took her for various subjects and would probably draw up a daily or weekly schedule of objectives for your daughter to meet. This kind of structure is often very successful and usually involves the child herself in determining what needs to be done. If no such provision is suggested, do not hesitate to make a fuss with the local authority, if necessary inviting your present school governors to complain. If some local authorities can provide proper support, there is no reason why others should not.

Problem Four

My 15-year-old son is taking his GCSE in seven or eight subjects this year. However, his French teacher says he should concentrate on all four Basic papers and not even bother with the four Higher papers. As I understand it, this will mean he cannot even obtain a grade of A, B, or C which he would need to go on to further or higher education. Can we force the school to enter him for all the papers?

Comment: The GCSE in modern languages tests speaking, listening, writing and reading at two levels, Basic and Higher, making eight papers in all. In order to gain a grade C, a candidate probably has to take at least six of the papers and do well in them. If the school is suggesting your son only takes the Basic papers, he may well have made a mess of the Higher papers in the mock exams. The school will judge, therefore, that he might do best to concentrate on getting maximum marks in the more simple Basic papers.

75

You have a number of choices. You cannot force a school to enter a pupil willy-nilly for anything you judge fit, but you can apply considerable pressure. However, you might have to consider paying for private tuition to bring him up to a higher standard. Alternatively, he may need to promise to make a special effort in French and, with help from his teacher, improve his work for the Higher papers. You would need to ask him and yourself whether an extra load might affect his chances of obtaining good grades in his other six or seven subjects, especially if there is a lot of course-work in these which might be inhibited if he had to spend a lot of time on French. If you press hard, the school may well agree to enter him for the other papers, but it might be better, if he needs a higher-grade pass in French, to consider taking the Basic papers this year and then resitting all the papers the following year to get a higher grade.

Problem Five

My 16-year-old daughter has a very incompetent maths teacher. He does not mark her work regularly and she says he does not really know as much as the other teachers. I have met him and, although he is only in his forties, he seems to have lost interest in his teaching. We do not want to make a fuss, but our daughter needs maths for her future career, so it is vital for her to do well this year.

Comment: Teachers are incompetent for different reasons, usually not just one single cause. Check how your daughter's school is organised, but there may well be a deputy head who is responsible for curriculum and possibly also staff development. Make an appointment to see this person, or if necessary the head, on a confidential basis, and spell out exactly what your daughter has told you. However, check first that you have the full facts, if necessary by consulting other parents about their children's views.

Do not be surprised if the person you eventually speak to at the school is fairly straight-faced about the matter. Even if there have been lots of complaints, professional courtesy forbids someone saying, 'Thank you for telling me, we've got the villain at last'. In any case, there may be many facts of which you are unaware. The teacher could have had some personal tragedy, like a broken marriage or ill health, and a school would have to take all these into account. The 1986 Education Act set up a formal system of teacher appraisal and if parents have regularly complained about this teacher, then that should be part of the appraisal. The school should certainly ensure that your daughter's work is marked more regularly and in the short term they may consider sharing the teaching of her class between two teachers to minimise the damage of one incompetent. If you are genuinely satisfied there is incompetence, then do not be deterred from taking the matter up in a sensitive but persistent manner with the head or deputy. It is your duty to do so and their responsibility to do what they can.

Problem Six

For some time now, a small group of unpopular parents has dominated things at my daughter's school. At one time they more or less ran the PTA and now they have got themselves voted on to the governors in some way. The latest shock came when the governors announced that they were proposing to 'opt out', something which I am not happy about. They held a ballot, but I know for a fact that several parents, opposed to the idea like me, never received ballot papers. Now the governors are saying that they have 'won' with only 50 per cent of the votes. Is this fair? Most parents around here do not seem to understand what the whole thing is about.

Comment: Several things have clearly gone wrong here, and parents have good grounds to object firmly. Firstly, a school which seeks to 'opt out', either because parents have demanded a ballot or because the governors feel that it is the right thing to do, must explain the reasons and implications fully to parents. This could be done by a circular letter or even by Press announcements. That apparently did not happen in this case.

Secondly, schools must keep a list of all parents eligible to vote in matters like this – and parents must be able to buy a copy of the current list at no more than the cost of production, probably a few pence only. It should be possible to see whether those who received no ballot papers were on the list. That said, however, more than a few schools have difficulty in finding out exactly who and where the parents of all their children are and some parents may even take the view that this is an invasion of their privacy. A school cannot be expected to make more than reasonable efforts to ensure that the voting list is complete and accurate.

For the ballot to be valid, at least 50 per cent of the parents must cast a vote. If fewer parents vote, the governors can either abandon the idea or hold another ballot within fourteen days. If they take the latter course, then a simple majority of those voting will suffice.

The size of the majority is trickier. In theory, a majority of one vote in favour is sufficient to carry the day, just as it is in Parliamentary and local government elections. However, any proposal to 'opt out' must ultimately be approved formally by the Secretary of State, and such a small majority might make him or her think twice, particularly if there were to be loud local protests.

The Secretary of State can also declare a ballot to be irregular or invalid and can require the governors to do it again properly. This seems to be necessary in this case.

Problem Seven

My son is very interested in becoming an engineer, like his uncle. Unfortunately, the craft, design and technology (CDT) teaching at his school is very poor. I have tried talking to the headteacher, who sympathises, but she says that there is little she can do as resources are limited and good teachers are hard to come by.

Comment: Unfortunately, the headteacher may be correct here. If so, it looks as if a transfer to a more suitable school is called for, and the headteacher would probably be willing to help in this.

However, if you feel that the problem is the school's complacency, an approach to the governors, either directly to the chair or via another governor, is the next step. The 1986 and 1988 Education Acts gave governors vastly more responsibility for what goes on in their schools, and you should not be put off by statements that they will 'consult the LEA' or whatever. They are now responsible with the head for teaching policy within the National Curriculum, and, very importantly, now have control over the school's budget. If, in fact, not enough money is being spent on CDT, the governors need to explain how such a decision came about. Parents can find out exactly how much is being spent on various aspects of the school's curriculum by looking at the financial statement which must be sent to them with the papers for the governors' annual meeting.

If such an approach fails to satisfy, then it is possible to write to the clerk to the governors asking for the matter to be put on the agenda for the annual governors' meeting. One can ask for a report on CDT teaching at the school, which should provoke full discussion of the issue.

It is necessary to word this very carefully, however. The annual meeting is not the place to mount attacks on (or to pat on the back) particular named teachers, and the chairman will quite properly immediately rule such things out of order. But *general* questions about, say, examination results in CDT or the amount of cash and time spent on it are quite in order.

Under the 1988 Act, governors can hire and fire teachers. In extreme cases, this may have to happen. They must also ensure that there is a proper appraisal system for all staff, including those who teach CDT.

The important point here is that most major decisions affecting schools are made at school level, and not, as they used to be, miles away at County Hall. Those responsible are, or should be, easily accessible to parents.

Problem Eight

I am getting increasingly alarmed by horror stories from my children about chaos in their school at lunchtime. I gather that fights are commonplace, that younger children are terrified and that there never seems to be a teacher in sight to supervise the children. Yesterday someone stole my son's sandwich lunch and he could not find anyone on duty to help.

Comment: This problem has been around in schools for years now, and there are few signs that a totally satisfactory answer is yet in sight. The contract to which teachers work does not *require* them to be around school at lunchtime or to supervise children then. Most teachers in fact *are* in school, however, preparing lessons, marking, running voluntary activities, but not patrolling the grounds and casting an eye on what is going on. Teachers did for many years volunteer to supervise children at lunchtime, but subsequently decided that a break then was their entitlement, just as it is everyone else's. The headteacher is responsible for setting up a supervision system at lunchtime, but probably without help from teaching staff.

For this reason LEAs employ welfare assistants to supervise pupils at lunchtime. This is usually paid as unskilled part-time work and top-flight recruits are sometimes hard to find. The thought of having to handle perhaps a couple of hundred boisterous teenagers for an hour may be a major disincentive!

A parent can do little more in this case than report the matter to the head. You might perhaps in some way organise an appeal to the staff to help out, but be ready to get a flat refusal. You could even approach the head about getting a rota of parents to help out at lunchtime, as already happens in some cases. Since the head carries overall responsiblity for pupils' safety, this might not get approval.

One suggestion which is being tried is to pay teachers additionally to supervise. Governors might look to their budget for this. However, even then, it is likely that the work might not appeal to teachers, who, after all, supervise children already all day.

Problem Nine

My son is a gifted linguist who has made great progress in learning French. Now I want him to learn a second language, preferably Russian, but there is no provision for any other language at his school.

Comment: Getting changes made to the curriculum of a school, provided that they are within the National Curriculum, is nowadays more feasible than it used to be, given that governors and the head together could agree a change and the LEA need not be involved. Languages other than French are spoken by millions of people and it is government policy that a range of languages should be taught.

Timing is the key to this. It is most unlikely that you will be able to get an additional teacher, unless by some miracle people are breeding happily in your area and the school is actually growing. This means that you will have to try to ensure that any teacher who is replaced can offer Russian. Keeping in close touch with your son's French teacher might give you inside information if a languages teacher decides to leave. When the time is ripe, approach the head first and then the governors. Remember, though, that there might be some 'knock-on' effect on the rest of the curriculum, so make sure you know exactly what is involved. It also helps, of course, to find other parents with similar interests. The school might consider employing a part-time teacher or investing in a self-instructional course.

Problem Ten

When we moved to our new town, we very much wanted to send our children to the new City Technology College (CTC). When we approached the principal, however, we were told that we did not live in the right area. Finding that a bit odd, we tried to use the LEA appeals system, but got nowhere at all.

Comment: When the government set up the CTC, the intention was that they should be substantially like other local comprehensives but for a strong technological bias in the curriculum and for financial support from industry. CTCs are not selective schools, like grammar or public schools, which have entrance tests to secure the best pupils they can, regardless of where they live. CTCs, like the other schools in their area, draw the vast majority of their students of all levels of ability from the area served by the college, although within that area they may give preference to pupils who show an aptitude for the curriculum on offer, and whose parents also show a commitment to it. Hence the statement that you live 'in the wrong area'.

For a number of very technical reasons, the DES classifies CTCs as independent schools, albeit with a number of important differences. The LEA appeals machinery for admission to schools applies only to schools maintained by the LEA, and as yet is not available in cases like yours.

Problem Eleven

We live very close to our child's school and are getting fed up with the noise and vandalism to our property virtually every day now at four o'clock, when school finishes and a thousand children come crashing down our road. I have tackled the head about this but he says that there is nothing he can do after four o'clock when the children have left the premises.

Comment: It would be beyond the power of man to keep a thousand children quiet after school. There is little you can do about that.

However, in other respects, the headteacher has got the situation wrong. It is a long-standing tradition that it is part of the job of British schools to try to teach good behaviour: teachers, as we saw earlier, are considered to be like parents and, like parents, are concerned with good behaviour.

The problem is: when and where does the school's authority stop and the parents take over? The answer which has been given by the courts is that anything a child does on the journey to and from school is the school's business. It does not matter how the child gets to school – the legal position is that a child could legitimately be punished at school for misdemeanours committed on the way there, even if accompanied by his or her parents. The same applies to any school bus.

This does not mean that the school is *responsible* for vandalism – but it does mean that the headteacher could throw his or her disciplinary weight behind trying to stop it. If the head is still unwilling to get involved, try the chairman of governors.

However, if the vandalism is severe, it might be wiser to turn to the police. Nowadays magistrates' courts can order parents of convicted vandals to pay the children's fines and compensation on top. Schools, on the other hand, have no powers to do this. If a school were to try to get a parent to pay you compensation under threat of going to the police, schools will fear it may come close to extortion or demanding money with menaces – not at all the desired outcome. Moreover, if you have reported a vandal to the school and the school has taken action, you may find that the police or magistrates take the view that the child has already been punished and are unhappy about punishing him or her twice. The risk, therefore, is that by involving the school you might make it impossible to get the compensation you want.

There is, incidentally, no *guarantee* that the magistrates will order compensation to be paid. They will judge each case on its merits.

Problem Twelve

Our son comes home from school with a great deal of information about sex, homosexuality and the like which we find quite distressing for his age. We think that children should be protected from all that. Is there anything we can do?

Comment: Most parents recognise that this is a touchy area and teachers try to deal with it sensitively. Sex education in secondary schools tends to be taught as an identifiable entity on the curriculum, which to some extent makes it easier to make adjustments to suit parents' wishes. This is simply not possible in primary schools, where teachers must inevitably answer children's questions as and when they arise – which is often! This is why the suggestion that parents should be able to remove their children from sex education has never been implemented and probably could never be. It would involve teachers having to say: 'Yes, Fred, I do know where you came from but your mummy and daddy do not want *you* to. . . !'

The law requires sex education to be given against the background of normal family life. Governors of schools are responsible for keeping an eye on their sex-education policy, and parents may complain to them if it is not adhered to.

Some concern was aroused in schools when Section 28 of the 1986 Local Government Act forbade the teaching of the

acceptability of homosexuality as a pretended family relationship, since it was feared that the section would inhibit full
discussion of the matter with pupils.

Homosexuality exists as a fact of life and common sense
tells us that there must be homosexually-inclined children in
schools. By law, all children are entitled to sex education –
was Section 28 intended to deny homosexual children part of
their rights?

The issue was cleared up by a 1988 Department of the
Environment circular (not from the DES incidentally, because
the Local Government Acts are administered by the DoE).
Objective discussions of homosexuality are not prevented, nor
is the counselling of pupils who may be concerned about their
sexuality. Nor does the section inhibit any teaching in the
field of health education or about AIDS.

An earlier DES circular recognised that schools cannot avoid
tackling issues of this sort: that remains the position in law.

Problem Thirteen

I would very much like to become a school governor, but I am
afraid that nobody would take much notice of me because I do
not know very much about the school as my daughter has
only just started there. I did not have much education myself,
although I did work in a bank at one time.

Comment: Being a school governor is not like being the boss
of a factory who knows all about the firm and sends out orders
to everyone. Headteachers are appointed as the experts in how
to run schools efficiently on a day-to-day basis, and governors
are not expected to take over headteachers' jobs.

Moreover LEAs, polytechnics and universities nowadays run
training courses for governors, not least because the job is far
more complicated and demanding than it used to be.

Governors are there to represent a common-sense layman's
view of things to the professional educators. A parent-
governor, for example, represents a view of how parents feel
about the school and all its works. This does not mean that
parent-governors are delegates who must pick up and argue

fiercely at meetings about every little grumble they overhear, but they must have a feeling for the *general* views of parents.

Having a governor who has worked in a bank could be a great asset to a school now that the financial policy for each school is decided by its governors – experience of working with perhaps quite large figures and a knowledge of simple book-keeping could be positive advantages. You could find out about being co-opted on to a governing body because you have this experience – contact the headteacher or the chairman of governors, whose name and address ought to be displayed at the school.

Problem Fourteen

My neighbour has collected several brochures from local secondary schools and believes that the best way to choose a school is to look at its examination results. What do you think?

Comment: Since the introduction of regulations under the 1980 Education Act, the law has required schools to publish their results in public examinations in school brochures. This may soon apply not only to GCSE, AS and A levels, but also to national 'bench-mark' tests based on the National Curriculum.

On one level, it can be said that examination results are a very crude measure of a school's success or failure. Few educationalists would disagree with that. But the results tell us only how school X compares with school Y in the year in which the brochures are published. Moreover, the public examinations mentioned above are taken at the ages of 16, 17 and 18, and tell us nothing about children's academic achievements at the age of 11. Most parents enter their children for secondary education at 11 and there is plenty of time in the next five years for schools and pupils to improve or deteriorate. Any headteacher can confirm that the departure of Mrs Jones from physics or Dr Smith from geography can wreak havoc overnight on examination results – and a brilliant replacement can restore them. Despite much propaganda to the contrary, the best evidence is that schools and teachers *do* make a critical difference to children's educational careers.

A more serious worry is that examination results say

nothing about whether schools cause their pupils to over-achieve or under-achieve. Although grammar schools enjoyed high public esteem (and the remaining ones still do), there was concern that some of them at least did not do as well by their pupils as the pupils deserved. Put another way, while it was indisputable that the examination results of the vast majority of grammar schools were superior to those of other schools available at the time, the strong suggestion remained that they could have done much better. In other words their pupils under-achieved.

Similarly, there are schools nowadays which work miracles with the most unpromising material. Their pupils may suffer every social handicap known yet, by brilliant hard work and skill, their teachers achieve remarkable results. For some of these children and their teachers, the achievement of two or three GCSE subjects is the equivalent of scaling Everest. It is an achievement for which these children and their parents are eternally grateful – yet such a school looks not very successful in the rank order of examination results. Good school plays, choirs, chess clubs, scouts and guides, sports teams and a host of other valuable activities do not figure in examination league tables.

Another question your neighbour should ask himself is: what happens if I choose a 'high-flying' school for Jeremy and poor Jeremy after a year or two is simply not up to the pace? Will his teachers know how to cope with him? Or (perish the thought!) will they encourage your neighbour to go elsewhere, lest Jeremy fouls up their excellent record in public examinations? Who are schools for?

On the other hand, in what is now called our 'credential society' exam results can be very important, in some cases the difference between obtaining a job and being unemployed. So should exam success be placed right at the top of a parent's list of criteria for choosing a school?

These are some of the questions your neighbour should ask himself. If the quality of education is judged only by examination results, a lot of hard work by teachers goes unrecognised and young Jeremy might actually be worse off. Would his parents, if they had to choose, prefer him to be a hard-working, pleasant and co-operative citizen or an uninteresting 'exam-passer'?

If, however, your neighbour is especially keen on examination results, the book *Choosing a State School* by Caroline Cox, Robert Balchin and John Marks (Hutchinson, 1989) has a whole section on the topic, showing how schools'exam results can be compared with each other, although we ourselves are not convinced of the value of such detailed arithmetical calculations.

Problem Fifteen

My son looks like being a keen violinist and has been taking private lessons. Now that he has started music lessons at school, I asked the headteacher whether violin lessons could be included. I remembered reading somewhere that education in school is provided free, so I assume that I should not pay.

Comment: The basic principle under the law is that education in maintained ('State') schools is provided by the taxpayers and parents should not, therefore, have to pay twice, through fees for example. (Parents of children at independent schools usually wince at this, because of course they *do* have to pay twice.)

Over the years, however, the system has collapsed under its own weight. As teachers have enthusiastically developed new curriculum activities, found even more interesting places further afield to visit with their pupils, enlarged the school orchestra, decided to teach engineering skills by renovating the school's battered minibus and so on, the system has had to say: thus far and no further.

Schools have reached the point where they simply cannot finance the expansion of activities like these any longer. The problems are invidious. In any school, not all the children who would wish to go on an educational journey can afford to do so. Does the school leave them behind? What if leaving them behind on this and other occasions handicaps their chances of success in examinations? The difficulties are endless.

As the law currently stands, LEAs must publish their policy

for charging in schools. They may still *not* charge fees, but they can, if they choose, charge for tuition in musical instruments.

They may not, however, charge for anything which is integral to an examination course. So if your child happens to be taking such an approved examination course and violin playing is part of it, then tuition must be provided free.

LEAs are entitled to charge for school journeys if they involve residential stays or long absences. Geography field-trips, trips to Germany for linguists and historical excursions are typical examples. The trouble here, of course, is that again not all parents are able to pay, with the result that in some schools educational visits and the like have to be drastically curtailed.

In some cases, LEAs and school governors may have welfare funds available to help families in difficulties, but this is not universal.

CONCLUSION

In this book we have tried to give a picture of how parents and teachers can work together harmoniously. Although the last section has been devoted to problems, we should not wish to finish with the suggestion that relationships between parents and teachers are invariably frayed. Numerous possible sources of friction and tension are defused every day in schools where positive efforts are made to establish and sustain an effective partnership between parents and teachers.

Parents who show an interest in their children's education can achieve much more than is apparent on the surface. It has been well known and documented for many years that children whose parents support them tend to do better in school than those whose parents do not. But those parents who make the effort can often help all children, not just their own. Parent-governors, for example, can secure benefits for the whole community by being on the governing body. Parents of one dyslexic who fight for better provision will make life easier for future generations, whose parents might not always be as persistent or might not have the self-confidence to take on what seems, from the outside, to be a powerful local authority.

We hope that this book has been of value to all parents concerned about their children's education, whether they become publicly active or not. Although there are now more second chances for people who do not succeed at their first attempt in our educational system, for most children their first chance will be their best one. Parents who help them make the best of it will not have wasted their effort.

INDEX